THE CHURCH
WITH THE GOLDEN ROOF

The Church with the Golden Roof

by Joe Powlas

HARLO   DETROIT

Library of Congress Catalog Card Number: 87-83048

ISBN: 0-8187-0103-X

Printed by Harlo Press, 50 Victor, Detroit, MI 48023

In Memory of

CLYDE GABBARD

who knew that one day I would write the book

and

DR. H.S. RANDOLPH
Board of National Missions
United Presbyterian Chruch U.S.A.

who asked that it be written

PREFACE

It was one of those days when everything had gone wrong. The old car would not start and, even if it had, there was a flat tire and no spare.

Slowly I walked down the hot, dusty road to the little Cow Creek post office to get the monthly bills for which there was no money.

Walking back up the road, I was the most dejected of all men. I had never known such lowness of heart, such sadness, such grief.

Why had I come to Cow Creek to begin my ministry? Why?

And then a question even more piercing—why had I even entered the ministry?

It was a long tiresome walk that morning and my steps were slow.

As the tears began to trickle down my cheeks, I looked across the creek to the little church on the hill.

The church had a golden roof! I had never seen such brilliance, such radiance! The splendor was unbelievable! The Cow Creek Presbyterian Church had a golden roof!

Suddenly, I realized that the roof was not golden. It was simply the sunlight falling upon an old dusty corroded tin roof, but, then, a great realization came to my mind. When

7

the light of God falls upon *any* object, no matter how old nor seemingly useless, it becomes beautiful.

I began to run, for I had never known such joy! What an honor and what a distinction! Joe Powlas was the pastor of a church with a golden roof!

INTRODUCTION

It is evening now and darkness is quickly approaching. For a little while I stand in the door of the old manse, looking up to the stately white church on the hill, the church where my ministry began. There is sadness in knowing that, when the door is finally closed, never again will I return.

The evening possesses a stillness and a quietness that is unusual. Somewhere in the distance one can hear the barking of a dog but, soon, even that becomes silent. I stand alone. Tears well in my eyes.

For a brief moment I want to reach out and capture, as an artist upon a canvas, the laughter of a people, the singing of a church, the happiness of a Christmas bag, the tears of a funeral; and I want this memory to be painted in flaming, colorful hues that can neither tarnish nor fade; for as I turn and walk away, the memories of this valley and of this people will be my only possessions.

The old apple tree in the yard—torn and twisted—has fallen to the ground. Once, tall and stately, it possessed strength and value. It, too, was a part of our valley. It, too, had been a part of our life. Now it lies broken and crumbled upon the ground and, in time, will be taken away and remembered no more.

For a few minutes I stand, remembering, and through the tears I see a valley in the mountains of Kentucky—they called it Cow Creek.

Junior Trosper, plow, and dog.

At the time of my early ministry he lived up the creek and he taught me much about the ways of Kentucky. First, one never made any derogatory remark about a man's dog.

"Joe, you can say anything you want to about what a man has but, never, never say anything about a man's dog. *Never!*"

I was to learn the truth of his words a few days later.

We all were up at Rudolph's Store just sitting, talking, and passing the time of day. Ed Moore joined us and we sat on the little porch talking about local politics. A car coming up the road suddenly made a screeching sound and a dog gave a distinct cry of pain. Ed immediately jumped up and ran to the middle of the road, stopping the car.

The frightened man behind the wheel got out. He was a complete stranger. We had never seen him before, and he trembled under the large hand of Ed Moore. Ed's words were stern and severe.

"You get out of here, and don't you *ever* hit another dog. Furthermore, don't you ever come back to this place."

The man, seeing the dead dog lying in the road, pulled out a handful of money and offered to pay Ed for his loss.

"Nope, I don't want your money. Just get in your car and git."

Hurriedly, the stranger got back in his car and drove out of sight.

"Ed," I offered apologetically, "I hate about your dog getting killed like that."

He smiled. "Twaren't my dog. I've never seen that mutt before."

Had that actually been Ed's dog there is every reason to believe that murder might have been committed on Cow Creek that day!

One Saturday morning, Clyde and I, Ed and several

other men, had gathered in the yard of the manse. On the spur of the moment it was decided to have a shooting match. A gun had been brought from the manse, some .22 shells secured, and a spot made on the trunk of the old apple tree. The joys of the creek were in playing Rook and competing in shooting matches.

We all shot, and Clyde won. We shot again, and Ed won. Pauline watched for a few minutes, then slowly started walking up to the church with a water bucket for the weekly cleaning.

Just being polite, I called for her to join us. The other men laughed at the thought of a woman entering the match. But Pauline calmly picked up the rifle, aimed, fired, and hit the target dead center.

"An accident. A pure accident!" someone said.

Pauline pointed the rifle toward the apple tree, pulled the trigger, hit the black mark dead in the center again, smiled, handed me the rifle, picked up her bucket, then walked on toward the church.

"I swear," Clyde said, "I just can't believe that a woman beat us!" She had—but the men never mentioned the fact to anyone!

One day we had gone to Lexington for supplies. It had been a long, hot, tiresome trip. The old car heated up. Strange smells came from the engine, as though oil was burning. I also had the feeling that the clutch would not last much longer. I was tired, hot, and disgusted.

As we approached the mouth of Cow Creek, the young man who had gone with me for the ride simply said, "Let's go swimming," just as Peter in the Bible had made the remark: "Let's go fishing!"

"We can't," I replied. "We don't have any bathing suits."

Calmly came the reply, "You don't need one. We'll just

go in without them. A lot of the boys here go in that way."

My better judgment told me that a Presbyterian minister simply did not go "skinny dipping" (Later I was to learn that during the Johnson Administration, this was done quite frequently at the White House pool!) but it seemed like a wonderful idea at the time.

Seeing my concern, he quickly added, "Besides, it's dark and no one can see us."

So, parking the car, we walked down to the edge of the river, pulled off our clothes—which we hid neatly in the bushes—then calmly, in the early darkness, walked out into the middle of the river. Whereas the air had been extremely hot and humid, the water was icy cold.

"Boy, this is freezing," he said, hitting the water.

"Let's swim up the river a little way, then get out," was my reply.

My thin frame soon became quite chilled. "I'm getting out," I cried. He had already gone several hundred feet up the river but, at my cry, turned and started swimming back downstream. And then it happened! Wilson Gabbard came over the bank with three girls (He was courting three at that time.) and a large paper bag and a cooler of soft drinks. Never have I been so surprised, startled, nor angry!

We were out in the river stark naked, and they were going to have a picnic! Our clothes were behind a rock in the bushes beyond where they were making camp.

They roasted wieners, drank pop, ate cake, laughed and joked and they had fun.

While upstream in the river, freezing, we were unable to get out. Shaking, and with teeth chattering, we watched the warmth and brightness of the fire on the shore. Never had I been so cold!

In time, Wilson and his companions consumed the food

13

and drinks and left. Then, weakly, two young men, turning blue and numbed by the coldness of the water, walked to shore to get their clothing.

Then and there it was decided that never again would I go swimming without the benefit of a bathing suit; but, then, I reasoned, it probably wouldn't matter, since in all probability I would die from pneumonia anyway.

In memory, the days at Sugar Camp now return. There was a little church at the head of the hollow. Each Saturday night I would climb into a Jeep (which belonged to the parish at that time), and drive the five or six miles from Booneville, picking up passengers along the way.

Since I had never driven a truck, church bus, or a Jeep before, the shifting of the gears from two wheel drive to four wheel drive became quite a problem.

One night we all started up the creek, the Jeep loaded with too many people crowded within, when suddenly there was a strange burning smell.

Cindy, a rather large lady, cried as she jumped out through the door and into two feet of mud, "My God, this thing is on fire!" Soon after, we all jumped.

Actually, the Jeep was *not* on fire. The clutch burned out. We walked the rest of the way in the mud and darkness; then later, a man drove us out of the hollow in the back of his pickup truck.

One night at one of the services I asked the small congregation at Sugar Camp what they wanted to sing. An elderly man from the back of the room immediately shouted, "Let's sing 'Amazing Grace.' "

Having grown up in a beautiful, stately, dignified Presbyterian church in North Carolina, I did not know, nor had I ever heard of "Amazing Grace." ("Amazing Grace," incidentally, is the most beloved hymn in Kentucky.)

Standing at the piano, my reply was simple. "I don't know 'Amazing Grace.' I can't play 'Amazing Grace.' What else would you like to sing?"

The old man in overalls on the back row called out, "I said, let's sing 'Amazing Grace.' "

My answer was kind but firm. "I don't know 'Amazing Grace,' but when I go back to the seminary I will try to find the music and next week we can sing your hymn. What else would you like to sing?"

One lady said, "Let's sing 'In the Garden.' "

I was relieved! "Good, turn in your hymnals to page sixteen. Stand, and we will sing all stanzas."

I took my place at the piano and we all started to sing "In the Garden," but from the back row there came a voice, both loud and clear,

"Amazing grace, how sweet the sound,
That saved a wretch like me.
I once was lost but now am found,
'Twas lost, but now am free."

It was always good to be back out of the hollow, for truthfully, the darkness and the loneliness of the church gave one a rather frightening feeling. Many tales had been associated with Sugar Camp. On one occasion some boys, as a prank, dug up a skeleton, put the skull on a long pole, then went from house to house, knocking on the doors. When the door was opened, all that could be seen was a skull, seemingly suspended in midair.

Though I loved the preaching and singing, and I loved the people, there was always that innate fear as we drove up the long, dark hollow.

15

One night, following the service, we had just about reached the main road when Addie said, "Joe, I hate to bother you but do you mind going back up to the church?"

My blood froze! It was late, the night was extremely dark, and most of our crowd had been deposited as we came back out of the hollow, which meant that only a few were left in the Jeep.

"Do you really *need* to go back to the church, Addie?" I asked.

"Yes, Joe, we left one of my younguns asleep back on the pew."

I turned the Jeep around. We went back up the long hollow and, sure enough, on the pew was the little boy who had fallen asleep during the service. His mother lovingly picked him up and carried him to the Jeep.

"I thought one of the other children had gotten him," she said simply.

His name was Landon McDaniel and he was a Baptist minister. I don't remember when or how we met, but I admired his casual and friendly attitude. We talked often. He was the kind of minister that could talk just as easily about coon dogs as about religion, about ginseng as about sin but, most of all, I liked his overalls and his chewing tobacco. He was one of the people—he was a Kentuckian! He talked like them, he acted like them, he was admired and respected— not only as a preacher but also as an individual.

The thought came to me that it was time I shed my Louisville Presbyterian Theological Seminary look. (I only wore a tie on Sunday, or for funerals or weddings. But I realized that in my ministry overall pants or overalls were never worn, nor were brogans.)

A pair of overalls were secured from Willie Cooper, a farmer here on Cow Creek, and some tobacco for chewing was bought down at Carl Sebastian's Store. The overalls made me think of my grandfather in North Carolina, who died when I was a child. He would have been proud to have seen me in overalls but, being a devout Baptist, he also would have been dismayed to have known that I, his own flesh and blood, was a Presbyterian. That was even worse than being a Democrat!

So, feeling a sense of freedom and a sense of joy, I proudly put on the overalls and, excitedly, I chewed the tobacco.

Shortly thereafter I experienced nausea, intense nausea. The overalls were a source of irritation and confusion! I never knew where to put my hands—nor could I walk comfortably.

Sadly, the great truth came. Joe Powlas could not be a Landon McDaniel but only a Joe Powlas; so once again I put on my old brown baggy pants, my old shoes, and feeling weak and dizzy, *my ministry continued as it had formerly been.*

Strange that, in these hours, I should remember incidents both frivolous and inconsequential.

I remember so well an old mule and a beautiful, young, black-headed girl by the name of Mary Ann. Earl and I had walked up the hollow to their home and, sitting astraddle the mule, she casually asked, "Wanna ride to the store with me?"

Of course I did, but she did not know that I had never been on a mule before. After much pushing and pulling, a tall, lanky, Presbyterian minister was seated securely on the old mule with the beautiful black-headed girl behind him. She put her arms around his waist to hold on, and it was then that he knew, as the Bible teaches, that heaven does begin on earth!

We started down the hollow, but the old mule was not very energetic, so I broke off a limb and laid this to the hind parts of the animal. Immediately we took off in high gear, and that mule ran like he was a part of the Kentucky Derby!

Just as we approached Gene Moore's house in full gallop, the belly band broke and we both hit the ground, with Mary Ann on top of me! The fall was most painful; my arms hurt, my legs hurt, my back hurt but, most of all, it hurt my dignity!

I walked up the road one day to visit a mother with a new baby. It was the Melvin Sebastian family, and everyone on the creek loved this family. They were nice, friendly and good, and they were most active in our church.

The child was several days old. "Bonnie," I asked, "what is the child's name?"

There was silence, then, smiling, she replied simply, "We haven't named her yet. Would you like to name her?"

What an honor! I had the privilege of naming a child. I was given the opportunity to name a newborn baby. I just couldn't believe it.

"You mean I can actually name your child?"

"Yes, name her anything you want."

I thought for a moment. There had been a beautiful girl down in North Carolina by the name of Lockie Hollander; so this became my choice.

"Let's name her Lockie."

"That's a real pretty name, Joe. Lockie it shall be!"

Lockie grew up within the church and became a beautiful woman, kind and sweet and good, just like her predecessor!

It was quite an honor for the minister "to take a night" with a family of the church. Always, when leaving, there would be the words, "Come and take a night."

This I did quite often, though I never quite understood why they always got up in the morning around four a.m.

18

and then sat in front of an open fire for two hours! Breakfast, ready on the table at six, consisted of fried chicken, ham, biscuits and gravy, eggs, and fried potatoes.

One night I had been invited up to Fred and Della Reynolds' to take a night and, of course, to have supper with them. There was sickness on the creek and it was necessary that a trip be made to Lexington with one of our members. Before going, I hurried up to Fred's and called from the car that a trip had to be made to Lexington but that we would hurry back just as quickly as possible.

When one goes to a hospital, not only is it ninety-three miles away but, usually, there are hours and hours of waiting as tests are made and questions are asked. We stayed all day at the University of Kentucky Medical Center and, not having had any lunch, it was my suggestion that we stop and get some hamburgers to eat before going home. In my intense hunger, I ate three and drank a chocolate milkshake!

Imagine my surprise when, arriving at ten-thirty that night, I found Fred and Della sitting out on the front porch waiting for me. Not only were they waiting but, no one, not even the children, had had any supper.

"We knew you would be hungry, so we waited for you!" One cannot imagine the love and compassion that I felt for those people. Without saying a word, I sat down and ate as though I had been starved for a week. They were never to know that every bite had to be forced down. That night there was no sleep, only tossing, turning, acute indigestion, and heartburn and the following day there was diarrhea.

And so Kentucky was to offer a young man a new life, a new way of thinking, incidents which were often unpredictable and unimaginable. Life was never dull!

His name was Snowball Abshear. He had grown children who were married, so when I picked him up one day as he walked along the road I was not surprised when he proudly said, "Joe, there's a new baby at my house!"

Thinking of the older sons and daughters, and I knew them all, I simply asked, "Whose is it?"

Startled, he replied, "My God, it had better be mine!" Then I remembered that, after his wife had passed away, he had married a young girl. She was the proud mother and he, of course, was the proud father!

The Bible states that there is a time to be born and there is a time to die, meaning that there is a time for every thing. There is a time to be helpful and, definitely, there is a time *not* to be helpful.

Returning from Cincinnati, I drove up Cow Creek about two-thirty one morning. Because I was so sleepy, it was difficult keeping my eyes open, but the manse was not far away. Then, at the Pet Wilson Curve, I noticed a car pulled over to the side of the road with the lights turned off. I immediately recognized the car, stopped, got out and walked over to the darkened car, asking, "Do you need any help?"

Startled and embarrassed, the boy stammered, "No, Preacher, thank you. I don't need any help." The couple straightened up and the boy started the car and drove off on up the road to another hollow. Neither of them came back to church for a long, long time!

I remember going down to the river one night to a place called "the Sag" with Herb Baker, who lived on the other side of Booneville. He was an excellent fisherman and he wanted to teach me the art of setting a trotline; so we set the line, built a fire in a bucket of sand and kerosene, then talked into the wee hours of the morning. The trotline was run, fish were caught, then fried. Cornbread was heated in an old black skillet, coffee made in a discarded pot and I ate as I had never eaten before. Kentucky was opening up an entirely new world to me, and I loved it more than I had ever thought possible!

As I stand here in these last moments, strange that I should remember so well the delicious strawberry ice cream made by Elsie McIntosh. Fresh strawberries from the garden, cream from the local cows, blended together by the expertise of one who, through the years, had mastered the art of cooking. No ice cream anywhere, at anytime, ever gave the taste of that made by Elsie!

Thousands of memories flood my mind. Why should I now remember an incident that once brought both humor and embarrassment? The potbellied stove in the sanctuary would be taken down during the summer and the hole in the ceiling stuffed with rags. This ritual was followed every year. One spring the only items that could be found were several pairs of long underwear which had arrived in a box so, taking a broom handle, I poked the white long johns up the hole in the sanctuary ceiling.

He was a guest minister, a Baptist, and he had been invited to be with us that Sunday but, as Baptists so often do, he preached way past my customary twenty minutes. Sitting in the back row I saw first the leg, then the flap, then slowly the rest of the white long underwear come through the hole —and I watched in horror as one pair, then the other dropped to the sanctuary floor.

The sermon, amidst giggles and laughter from the congregation, came to a sudden halt, and the visiting minister never came back again.

During my ministry I always wanted to hear the physical voice of God. What a wonderful experience if I, as Moses and Abraham and Noah, could commune with God, actually face to face. This is the dream of every minister: to hear God speak directly to him!

One day, tired and discouraged, I came on the hill, got out of my car and and started walking toward the manse. From the heavens there came a deep resonant voice, "Hello there!"

It did not come from the ground, it came from the sky! In disbelief, I stopped. At long last, my dream was coming true and my prayer was being answered.

Again the voice spoke, "Hello there."

There was great joy within me. Joe Powlas, at Cow Creek, Kentucky, was receiving a voice. I was not in New York at 475 Riverside Drive. I was not in Pittsburgh at 524 Penn Avenue, nor was I at the Louisville Theological Seminary. I was at Cow Creek and I was hearing a voice from the heavens.

The voice spoke again. I looked up into the sky, but was greeted by the intense sun. My vision was blurred by the light.

"What are you doing down there?"

Now, that puzzled me. If the voice belonged to God, then surely He knew what I was doing down here. Then I saw a movement on the telephone pole. The voice was coming from a black man, perfectly silhouetted against a black telephone pole. The repairman was simply being friendly. It was he who had been speaking to me all along.

Weakly, I waved my hand in greeting. Then, with great disappointment a bewildered minister walked into the manse. Maybe the voice was to come later, after years of experience and trials and tribulations.

Strange that in this hour I should remember so well helping Gene Moore weed his tobacco bed, and in so doing I pulled up every tomato plant that the man had.

I remember going over to Bill Bowling's early one Sunday morning to tell the family that his grandson, Andy, just back from the Marines, had been killed in an automobile crash just outside of Booneville.

I remember a get-well card from the young people addressed to "The best *pasture* a church ever had!" and how could I forget the little boy calling, asking if he might go with me to *my surprise birthday party* the following night.

I remember so well hearing the telephone ring every Sunday morning when a small kid would call.

"Hello," he would say, and I would answer, "Hello."

Then he would ask, "Who is this?"

My answer always would be, "This is Joe."

"What time are you going to pick us up?" referring to the church van, which I then drove.

"A quarter to ten," would be my reply.

"Bye, see you later."

This conversation happened every week and the words never varied. Always they were the same.

One Sunday the little boy called as usual. "Hello," he said.

"Hello," I replied.

"Who is this?" he asked.

I paused for a moment. I had on a white shirt, a black tie and a suit, so my answer for once was different. "This is the Reverend Mr. Powlas."

"Oops, wrong number," he said, and immediately hung up. A few seconds later the telephone rang again.

As a minister, how well aware I was of prayer! Tennyson wrote, "More things are wrought by prayer than this world dreams of!" And prayer was to become a constant source of strength and of power and, occasionally, of surprise!

The Reverend John Turner and I were returning from a

meeting of Presbytery in Stanton. While driving along Highway Eleven we were suddenly startled by the radiator getting hot. Immediately I pulled the car over to the side of the road. John and I got out, and John raised the hood to inspect the damage.

A beloved Presbyterian minister in this area, he was ending his ministry as I was beginning mine. We stood together by the side of a lonely road with a broken-down car. "Joe, you have a broken fan belt!"

We were miles from Beattyville (the nearest garage), and home. It was getting dark and there was the possibility that few cars would be travelling that late in the evening. As I was to do so often in my ministry, with eyes wide open and head erect, there was a silent prayer. "Lord," I whispered, "please help me. I need Thy help."

Within three minutes a truck passed and, although we made no attempt to stop the vehicle, it pulled to the side of the road and a young man got out and walked toward us.

"Got problems?"

"Sure have," I answered. "Broken fan belt."

He looked at my car, smiled, then walked back to his truck and returned with a fan belt and a few tools.

"It's not new, but it will get you home."

Quickly, he put the fan belt on the car, refused to take any pay, and was on his way.

John and I stood looking at each other, unable to believe our good luck. Then silently, we both got back into the car and headed for Booneville, well aware that it was the Lord who had provided.

But prayers were not always answered. There was to be a special prayer, prayed daily during my later ministry, that one beloved by me would unite with the church. Though I prayed fervently, it did not happen as I so badly wanted.

24

So many memories race before my eyes. It is as though for a few minutes I am trying to relive a lifetime. Desperately I reach out, pulling to me the years which have brought so much happiness and so much joy; and my prayer is that God, for a little while, will not take these memories from me.

1

The work at Cow Creek began in 1910 when two Presbyterian women—one from Pennsylvania, the other from New Mexico—came to our valley and founded the Athenia Academy. Presbyterians have long been interested in education and, at that time, there was a desperate need in Owsley County for additional schools and teachers. Through their efforts a large building was erected and this became the dormitory. The school building was built across the ravine. Children would come and spend the week then return home for the weekend. The work was supported by the Board of National Missions, United Presbyterian Church, USA, 475 Riverside Drive, New York, through which we acquired supporting churches. They became interested in our work and provided both financial support and material blessings, as needed. Frequently, I spoke to church audiences in Ohio, Virginia, Pennsylvania, Indiana New Jersey, and New York, giving my interpretation of the work of our church in Owsley County, Kentucky; and members of these churches would, in turn, visit our church, individually and in youth groups.

Over the years visitors came often.

I vividly remember our first visitors and I feel that they will long remember Cow Creek.

The early days were extremely difficult and, as is the case

with many ministers, my ministry began with very few material possessions. My first desk was a ping-pong table. My first filing cabinet was a pasteboard box.

In January I received a letter from Indiana. It was from several lady members of a supporting church who had heard of our work in Cow Creek and of Joe Powlas. They were requesting permission to come down the following summer for a visit. The reply was, of course, "Come on down," and, to my knowledge, no further correspondence was ever received.

On a beautiful day in late August, the men on Cow Creek were busy in the tobacco fields. I went from home to home, lending a helping hand as best I could, and at night I delivered a sermon at a revival which was being held at the Indian Creek Church. I left early the following morning and did not get home until late at night. The manse had not been cleaned for over a week. Dirty dishes were piled high in the kitchen sink, floors unswept, and papers were scattered in every room. Everything was in chaos.

The next day I helped Gene Moore, and how well I remember the wonderful dinner Lexene prepared—pork chops, mashed potatoes, green beans, and peach cobbler pie. We finished cutting Gene's tobacco field in the morning and in the afternoon we all went down to Carl Stepp's to help harvest his crop.

About four o'clock Gene Moore let me out of his pickup truck in front of the manse. I walked, so tired, from the main road to the manse, the happiest I had ever been in my entire life.

Truly, I was the most blessed of all men!

I loved my work, I loved the church, I loved the people. This was *exactly* what I felt God had wanted me to do, and I was grateful for His blessings.

So, in great joy, slowly my steps led me up the little hill to the manse. Suddenly I froze in my tracks!

There were six women, sitting on six suitcases, on the front porch of the manse. Six women, and each of them infuriated.

One woman walked toward me, pointing a finger, "Young man, could you please tell us where we might find the Reverend Joe Powlas?"

If only the earth had swallowed me up at that moment, what a blessing it would have been.

My clothes were filthy, my shoes were muddy, and I was covered with tobacco gum. Barely audible, I stammered, "I'm Joe Powlas."

She paused, looked at me, then stammered, "I don't think you understand! We want the *Reverend* Joe Powlas."

Slowly my hand was uplifted to hers. My weak, embarrassed smile assured her that her quest had ended, and, for a few moments, there was complete silence.

Suddenly, laughter reigned. Although Reverend Joe Powlas was not what they had expected, at last he had arrived. I graciously greeted the six tired and hungry women. They entered the manse and it was no time before the dishes were washed, the floors were cleaned, and an excellent supper was prepared from the potatoes and flour and the few scant items left in the refrigerator. That night one of the six women preached at the revival.

They remained for several days and all had a wonderful time. Though none of them ever returned to Cow Creek, through the years they supported our work through Christmas gifts and clothing.

Her arrival was the event of the year. She had been a generous contributor to our work at Cow Creek. Weeks prior to her coming, floors had been mopped and waxed, windows cleaned, the yard carefully mowed and trimmed. Anxiously, we awaited her coming.

When the long black Cadillac, driven by her chauffeur, drove up on the hill, I was at the door, ready to meet our special guest for the first time.

Everything went well. We visited two churches, had lunch at the manse, and she seemed favorably impressed until, during lunch, I made a statement that startled her.

The conversation had been about Sunday activities. I stated that, after church services on Sunday, I would go home, change clothes, and play softball.

"Mr. Powlas, you mean . . ." she chose her words carefully, ". . . you mean, *you* play softball on *Sunday?*"

"Yes," I answered triumphantly. "Three games."

Her face whitened. Her words became stern and cold.

"Well, I certainly don't approve of that. First of all, I don't approve of ministers playing softball. They are men of the cloth; and I find it even more repulsive that you play on *Sunday.* You will never hear from me again!"

We ate in silence. I thought about all the good times we had had during the summer months, remembering that the boys who played softball had, as a rule, been in church on Sunday morning.

"What do the young people in *your* church do on Sunday afternoon?" I asked.

She did not answer immediately, hesitating a few seconds. When she spoke, her voice was almost inaudible. "We have no young people in my church."

An elderly lady who was very wealthy, she played an important role in the life of her church, having much influence and monetary power; but, sitting there at the end of the table, she looked so lonely and sad. I hoped that she might smile, but such was not to be.

30

She departed shortly thereafter, and, true to her word, I never heard from her again.

I became chairman of the Foreign Missions Committee in presbytery, and in this capacity learned that missionaries from Korea, on furlough, would visit our church at Cow Creek, Kentucky.

The Session gave approval that an offering would be taken to help pay their expenses, and they would stay at the manse for their one night visit.

Never having met any foreign missionaries, I became excited over the prospect. At one time I, too, had planned to become a missionary, hoping to go to India. It had been my dream for a long, long time; but, I reasoned, foreign missionaries were no different than home missionaries. Both labored in the vineyards of the Kingdom, and both grew weary and tired, having difficulty in making ends meet.

Our visitors turned out to be an older couple, who had aged gracefully. Her hair was just the right color and beautifully styled. Their clothing was expensive.

The offering for their expenses was taken up and given to them prior to their introduction to the congregation. I noticed a particular elderly man putting five dollars into the collection plate. This, to him, was an awful lot of money. After the service I considered returning the money to him, but reasoned that the Lord had already accepted his money, and it just did not seem right to take from the Lord.

As our visitors spoke to the congregation, I realized that their lives were not as I had thought them to be. Missionaries in Korea had servants: servants to draw their water; servants to clean their house; servants to get their mail; servants to wash their clothes; and servants to cook their meals. After listening for fifteen minutes, I came to the startling conclusion that the servants did everything except *preach*.

31

It was fortunate for them that the offering had been taken before their presentation. Otherwise, they probably would not have received a cent!

Their overnight stay at Cow Creek turned out to be a rather unforgettable experience.

Quenton Callahan had the reputation of being the best farmer on Cow Creek, and one of the best in Owsley County. He grew the best tobacco, the largest potatoes, raised the finest hogs, and without a doubt, produced the most potent manure in our entire area.

Quenton had spread his fields with manure that day and the temperature rose, unexpectedly, to over one hundred degrees, making it extremely difficult for one to breathe—so pungent was the aroma.

There were no air-conditioners, or fans at the manse. The windows were simply raised, and the breeze cooled the manse sufficiently as it passed through.

I was most apologetic about the atmospheric conditions, but, of course, there was nothing that could be done. Had I asked Quenton, prior to their coming, to delay spreading the manure for several days, I am sure he would have obliged. But, being unaware of his time schedule, nothing had been said.

I baked a ham and an apple pie for supper, but the visitors did not feel like eating. I noticed that the lady missionary frequently took pills from a little bottle and drank a lot of water.

There was only one bedroom in the manse, so I slept on the couch downstairs, pitifully aware that the temperature upstairs was even hotter, and the smell of manure even stronger.

The visiting missionaries slept little that night. Most of their time was spent in arguing or complaining.

"He doesn't have a window shade. How on earth am I going to undress?"

"No one will see you out here. You are at Cow Creek, Kentucky. Remember?"

"I can't breathe. I simply can't breathe. That horrible odor. I am suffocating."

"Let's get out of here, right now. Let's not wait until morning."

"Darling—shut up! If I *knew* how to get out of this God forsaken place, we would leave right now; but I don't have the faintest idea how to get back to Lexington."

The aromatic, pungent smell of the manure reached out from the fields and fell across the valley, penetrating every crack and every corner—especially the nostrils of our foreign missionaries from Korea.

They left hurriedly the next morning without even saying good-bye.

I received a letter stating that the Princeton Theological Choir was coming to Cow Creek, Kentucky, during their concert tour. We could hardly believe such wonderful news. What an honor! The Princeton Theological Choir would sing in the Cow Creek Presbyterian Church! We wondered how, and why, we were chosen? Excitedly, we began to plan, and make ready for their coming.

Finally the great day arrived, and that evening our little church was filled to capacity.

It was an inspirational program, and they sang to absolute perfection. Their repertoire included compositions by Bach, Vivaldi, Mendelssohn, Franck, and Handel.

Our congregation, though polite, was not enthusiastic. Nor did I sense any great appreciation for so great an event. As the people slowly filed out of the church, I asked an old man in overalls how he liked the presentation.

"Frankly, Joe," he answered sternly, "I had just as soon have heard a cow bellow."

His comment had a lot of validity. I went to the conductor and explained that, for people of the city—for people of musical knowledge—Mendelssohn, Bach and Handel was an excellent presentation, but country and mountain people would be more uplifted by familiar gospel hymns and spirituals. Being a versatile choir, they immediately changed their repertoire to include spirituals, folk songs, and several of the more familiar hymns. Equally as important, the conductor seemed grateful for my suggestion.

Through the years a strong fellowship developed between many of our local people and our visitors. Such a fellowship existed between Clay and Sarah Chandler, up on Crane Fork, and the Lesnett sisters, Grace and Sarah, from Bridgeville, Pennsylvania.

They were all visiting Cow Creek one summer, together with Lew and Peg Hays, from Washington, Pennsylvania, and Margaret Ronaldson, from the Board of National Missions in New York. Clay and Sarah sent word for all of us to come up to their place for a home-cooked chicken and dumpling supper. Grace Lesnett dearly loved chicken dumplings and, more especially, persimmon pie.

We were all overjoyed at the invitation.

Early that afternoon Margaret Ronaldson went upstairs in the manse to dress for our evening supper. It took her a full three hours! We were all eager and waiting when she emerged—in full splendor; high heels, Fifth Avenue tailored-suit, beautiful hat, matching handbag and gloves. We stood in awe!

The Chandlers lived at the head of the Crane Fork hollow. Part of the road was in a creek bed, which was rocky and rough. I had asked Archie Lee Gabbard if he would come by and take us up in his pickup truck, for there was no possible way I could take my car.

Archie Lee arrived with his truck at the appointed time. I had forgotten it was Wednesday—Sale Day over in Lerose. Archie Lee had, indeed, been to the sale, and in the back of his truck was the largest sow hog I had ever seen.

We had no choice but to make the best of a bad situation. We put the two elderly ladies in the cab of the truck with Archie Lee, and Peg, Lew, Margaret and I climbed into the back of the truck with the sow. Every so often the hog would look up quizzically at Margaret in her beautiful outfit, and grunt. We made the five mile journey without incident, but never in my life had I laughed so much. Peg, Lew, Margaret, and I, all in the back of that pickup truck! We laughed all the way up the hollow and—after a bountiful meal of chicken and dumplings and persimmon pie—all the way back to the manse.

They were from Pennsylvania, from a large wealthy church. He was pitiful and nervous and reminded me of a small child who had been discarded and left alone, who was only now feeling the pain of abandonment. I will never forget the day they came to the manse—nor will I ever forget the sadness and fear showing in his deep blue eyes.

She was a very large woman, endowed with an extra-large bosom. In one of the textbooks in high school there had been a picture of a Sherman tank and, as she talked on and on, that picture kept flashing in my mind.

"Sit down," she shouted—immediately upon entering the manse. Obediently, he sat down.

"I really have been most fortunate . . . blessed in many ways . . . I am President of the Women's Association . . . I belong to our Garden Club which, incidentally, is most exclusive . . . I sing in the choir . . . I am an Elder in First Church," she rambled on, endlessly.

Her husband remained silent, sitting meekly with his fingers intertwined. My next question was directed to him. "What is *your* profession?" I asked.

"In college, I majored in . . ." He was rudely interrupted by the sharp and stern command, "Shut up!"

Then, turning to me, she continued. "I run our business which, I assure you, is a full time job . . . We have other businesses which I must also direct . . . It is so hard to find adequate and well-trained help these days . . ." She just talked and talked and talked. I, like her husband, simply sat and listened, unable to make either comment or suggestion.

Turning to her husband, she commanded, "Go out to the car and get those pictures on the back seat. We simply *must* show Reverend Powlas our lovely home and our three French poodles."

They were there for several hours. Never once did he speak, but she talked incessantly—about garden life; the work of the church; about her father, who had founded the family business; about the French poodles and how intelligent they were; and finally about politics. As she continued to talk I found myself wondering why these two had ever married. Had they actually been in love at one time, or had he married her for her money and security? Was he ever allowed to make a decision, or enter into a conversation?

Finally, after what seemed an eternity, she announced that they really must go.

"Go back up to the church and get a bulletin," she ordered her husband. "I want to take one to the Women's Association back home." Obediently, meekly, he started.

"Wait! Let me go," I interrupted. "I have to lock the church and if I go now, it will save me a trip later on."

I left them and hurried to the church for the bulletin. It took only a few minutes, but when I returned they were already sitting in the car with the motor running.

The woman glared at me angrily—angrier than anyone I had ever seen before. Her beady black eyes darted at me. "Young man, if that was your idea of a joke . . . You . . . You're sick!"

Quickly, she threw the gearshift into reverse, turned the car around and started over the hill. At that moment, I managed to catch a glimpse of the man's face. He was laughing uproariously—I mean really laughing. He raised his hands, cupped them together in the Victory sign, and there was happiness and joy written all over his face.

Why had she left in such anger. Then, almost immediately, I realized what had happened!

Women usually like to use the bathroom before leaving the house and she *had* gone to the bathroom! Therein was the answer to her anger.

For a long time I had wanted a brown commode seat. I had even gone to Lexington to purchase one at the Sears store, but the price had been higher than I expected. The only logical thing to do was to paint one myself. So, a quart of brown enamel paint had been bought, and that morning— unaware that visitors were coming—the toilet seat in the bathroom had been painted. Unaware of my recent project, the lady had sat down on a still wet, and extremely sticky, freshly-painted brown toilet seat!

The incident had caused her husband to laugh, and I knew it put a little joy into his otherwise joyless existence. With that knowledge as my consolation, I did not mind the two hours it took to re-sand and re-paint my smudged, brown, toilet seat.

A telephone call came from a friend stating that, at long last, she had found the perfect wife for Joe Powlas. I jumped three feet high at the welcome news and immediately started making plans for their arrival.

The manse was cleaned, and everything was placed in perfect order. Here I was, a young minister, waiting in great anticipation to meet the girl who perhaps was to become the future Mrs. Joe Durwood Powlas.

Just what was my conception of the ideal wife? After all, the statement had been made that she was "perfect." A minister's wife must be intelligent, but not haughty; beautiful, but not egotistical; sweet, but not sugary; fragile, but strong as an ox; and, finally, filled with love and compassion. She would wear a dress, hat, gloves and high heels, looking like Deborah Kerr or Joan Fontaine.

Eagerly, almost unable to breathe, I awaited their arrival.

At long last, the car from Indiana arrived. My friend emerged first, followed by the ideal woman who my friend presumed would move into the Cow Creek manse, and become the wife of the community's minister.

Her name was April. Her hair was done-up in curlers and was covered by a large blue kerchief. She weighed at least 300 pounds, and the overall pants she wore bulged painfully at the seams.

Before any welcome could be extended, April ran and embraced me warmly.

She smiled. "I just wish we could have brought the children with us. They would love Cow Creek."

"Children?" I asked weakly.

"Five," she answered, triumphantly. "You will love them. Three boys and two girls."

As was the custom, they were given the one bedroom

upstairs as I planned to spend the night on the couch in the living room.

Her large blue eyes followed my every move and, like a small puppy who follows his master, she followed my every step.

Even in the bathroom one was not safe. Although she had knocked, she had not waited for an answer and promptly entered. Luckily, I was just shaving.

"Here, let me help you shave," she offered, trying to take the razor from my hand. "I used to shave my late husband all of the time. He loved it." Politely, I replied that I was actually more comfortable shaving myself.

That afternoon, April wanted to go up the hollow for a walk. She wanted to climb to the top of the mountain to get a better view of the creek. She wanted to see how many different trees we could find. She wanted to see if per chance we might see a fox or a groundhog. Tactfully, my reply was that a sermon had to be prepared for a funeral the following day. Thus, gracefully, her invitations were declined.

That evening, after visiting the funeral home, the girls decided they would go to bed early and give themselves more rest for the return trip home the following day. I had just retired for the night when, about eleven o'clock, footsteps could be heard creeping down the stairs—slowly, one at a time. Since the boards squeaked under the weight, there was a presumption on my part that the person coming down the stairs was quite heavy. Quickly, and silently, I crept from the couch and tiptoed to the closet under the stairs. I opened the closet door very carefully. Then closing the door tightly behind me I crawled to the farthest end and there, in total darkness, I huddled with my arms around my knees.

The steps approached the couch, paused for a few minutes, then went from one room to the other—even going out on the porch before returning to the bedroom upstairs.

That was the only time in my life that I ever slept in a closet all night with my arms folded around my knees.

The women left the next morning, but not before consuming a huge breakfast. Their departure was in a lackadaisical manner.

After the car had disappeared over the hill, I sat for a long, long time on the front porch, a little sad and remorseful that the girl of my dreams, with high heels, wide-brim hat and white gloves, had not materialized. I had looked forward so much to meeting my Deborah Kerr.

And so, through the years, they came. They came from Pennsylvania, New York, Indiana, Ohio, Tennessee, Michigan, New Jersey, Washington, D.C., Virginia, Maryland, Massachusetts, Kansas, Illinois, Florida, and Kentucky.

Some stayed overnight, but most visited for only an hour or two. Yet, there were two visitors who *never* came—and I have the feeling that they never will.

There was a time in the life of Cow Creek when we bitterly fought the construction of the proposed Booneville Reservoir. Everyone, except those at the head of the creek, would have had to move from our beloved valley. The manse would have been forty feet under water! The Corp of Engineers fought to build the Booneville Reservoir, and we here on the creek fought to save our homes and our church.

We met periodically and planned our strategy. We organized, held meetings, went to Washington to appear before subcommittees, wrote letters and sent telegrams. We never referred to the project as the Booneville Reservoir. It was always, simply "the *dam*."

"Have you heard anything about the *dam*, Joe?" people would ask.

One day a call came from an elderly couple. Enroute to Florida, they had stopped in Cincinnati for lunch.

The caller said, "We have heard so much about Cow Creek and about Joe Powlas. We are heading to Florida for the winter. When we noticed on our map that Booneville was not far out of our way, we decided that we just had to meet you." He paused for a few seconds. "Do you have any plans for this evening?"

Without thinking I hurriedly replied, "Only a *dam* meeting at seven o'clock."

The man said, "Oh," then hung up. They never came by, nor did they ever call again. I have no idea who they were nor where they live. I have never in my life used profanity but, alas, there probably is one couple out there somewhere who believes that Joe Powlas is well-versed in cursing.

During the early days, while the schoolhouse was still being used as a schoolhouse (it was later to become the Summer White House), youth groups stayed at the manse, and this often created chaos. Although it was a large building—once a dormitory—there simply was not enough room within the manse to house twenty people. My bedroom was used by the counsellors and I slept, periodically, in the study; in the living room; on the front porch; or in the back room of the church. Later, I spent my nights at Clyde and Lucy's where I slept upstairs in their spare bedroom.

I could never get adjusted to the groups. It was difficult for me to go into the kitchen for a peanut butter sandwich only to find bags and bags of groceries everywhere.

One day a couple came on the hill to get married. I needed the *Book of Common Worship,* which contained the marriage ceremony, and the last place I remembered seeing it was in my bedroom where, one night lying in bed, I decided to memorize the marriage vows. Hurriedly, I ran into the bedroom to find the book, only to find two women undressing. I am not sure which of us were the more surprised. Their screams startled me; so quickly, I jumped into the bathroom and pulled the door closed behind me. Immediately, there came forth a piercing scream, even louder and more terrifying than the first, and an elderly lady started throwing bottles and bars of soap at me.

It took me a long time to recover from that embarrassment.

There was one couple and one occasion that brought me much happiness and joy, and that was the arrival of Al and Marcella Coates and their children, Steven and Sharon, from Penfield, New York. I had long awaited their arrival, for it had been through their individual efforts and the efforts of their church—the Penfield Presbyterian Church—that I had received a brand new Jeep!

The Reverend Donald McFerren, whom I had learned to know while he was at The Fifth Avenue Presbyterian Church, in New York, called one day.

"Joe, I am still in New York state, but I have changed locations and churches. I am now at the Penfield Presbyterian Church in western New York."

We talked for several minutes then, abruptly, he asked, "What do you need at Cow Creek?"

My first response was Christmas gifts for my congregation, since Christmas was not too far away.

"We want to share in both Foreign and National Missions," he said. "For Foreign Missions we are working toward securing an operating table for a mission in Africa, and I wondered what you needed at Cow Creek. Your needs would be our National Missions project."

42

I was completely astonished.

"Don, what price range are we talking about? A few dollars? A hundred? A thousand? Give me *some* idea as to the limits."

"There is no price range. There is no limit. Whatever you need! That is what we will set as our project—our goal."

My mind suddenly went blank! There was no price range? No limit? What did we really need? In boldness, my answer surprised even me.

The day before I had conducted the funeral for Regina Robinson at the funeral home. Originally the funeral had been planned for the Indian Creek Church, but ice and snow surrounding the church made it too dangerous for our older people to attend; so the decision was made to have the service at the funeral home, where the roads would be safe and clear.

On the way to the funeral home, however, in Booneville, in front of Charles Long's garage, my car slid off the road and into a ditch. There was no time to call a wrecker. I had a funeral to conduct in less than twenty minutes; so, with Bible in hand, I simply left the car and started walking. Within a few minutes a man in a four-wheel drive truck came by, stopped, picked me up and drove me out to the funeral home. After the service, Dick Searcy drove me home in his four-wheel drive vehicle.

So if there was no price range, no limit, my answer was easy.

"A Jeep, Don! I need a four-wheel drive Jeep."

"That sounds great, Joe. A great project. I have no idea how long it may take to buy a new Jeep—perhaps years—but that will be our project for National Missions."

Shortly thereafter a letter came from Al Coates, who was chairman of the Missions Committee. He asked for certain information which I supplied, and then there were numerous other letters and telephone calls.

Al worked hard on the project. He adopted the slogan, "A Jeep for Joe," and placed posters throughout the church.

It was first estimated that it would take *at least two years* to raise enough money to buy a new Jeep, but under the direction and encouragement of Al and Marcella Coates the money was secured in less than *six months!*

It all seemed like a dream. It was too good to be true! "A Jeep for Joe" had become a reality and, on a Saturday in February, I flew up to Penfield and, during the Sunday morning service, the keys were presented to me by a smiling Al Coates.

What impressed me far more than their ability to raise the money for a new Jeep in less than six months time was the fact that they, the Penfield congregation, sat on metal folding chairs in the sanctuary and the roof of the church was badly in need of repairs. There were buckets and pails located in strategic places throughout the building; and yet, in all of their need, they had given me a brand-new Jeep.

Arvis and I drove the new Jeep from New York back to Kentucky, and you could not have found a happier minister anywhere in the Presbyterian church than the one from Cow Creek, Kentucky!

When Al and Marcella arrived in Cow Creek it was a moment of joy—and of gratitude. Their stay was for several days and, during that time, we played tennis on the new tennis courts which had been built at the County Park just outside of Booneville. We drove the Jeep up in the hollows, where Al and Marcella made rubbings from the old headstones in the cemetery at Courtland. Through mud, creeks, ruts and hollows, the new Jeep rolled merrily on its way.

Not long afterwards we were saddened to learn that Al was seriously ill. His illness, thought at first to be arthritis, was later diagnosed to be cancer. I spoke to him at the hospital and he seemed confident and cheerful—the same vibrant Al who had so successfully raised the money for the Jeep and played such a mean game of tennis, but a few days later Marcella called, stating that Al had passed away.

While at Cow Creek and during his illness, Al and Marcella both started painting with watercolors. They would paint scenes from slides and pictures, and specialized in the painting of scenes containing old barns.

Not only had I received the wonderful gift of the Jeep, but also two beautiful watercolor paintings of the Cow Creek Church and of a county road leading up the hollow at Crane Fork.

Those who had given so generously of their time and of their financial blessings could never know of my gratitude, nor of my love, nor of my deeper commitment to the Kingdom of God. Through their trust and their concern there was a deeper sense of the awareness of unused strength, but even more importantly, a feeling of humility.

She was a beautiful person, from Duncan Falls, Ohio and she and her family visited Cow Creek often during my early ministry.

The poem "I Will Not Doubt" by Lois Torbert Dilley was used many times during the years of my ministry; and each time I read it, strength and consolation was given to a lonely, troubled minister.

Although my ship came home with broken sails,
And cherished dreams seemed shattered at my feet;
Yet, now I know the triumph of His Power;
And there is neither failure nor defeat!

For God, who made the ship, and set it forth,
Into the tempest, to withstand the gales,
Knows what high courage kept the craft alfoat,
And understands the torn, and broken sails.

He understands the battles that were there—
The adverse winds, that threatened to defeat,
He understands the stormy days, and fair;
The rocks—the shoals—the treacherous, hidden reefs,

And I can trust the Power of Him, who brought
Calm and assurance, from the stormy blast;
And I can trust the Love of Him who brought
My storm-tossed Vessel, into port, at last!

2

Weddings are always a great joy and, through the years, weddings have been most eventful occasions in the life of the church and in our community. In the early days, I recorded all marriages and funerals, which were carefully kept in a little black book; but somewhere along the way the book was lost so I have no idea how many funerals I have conducted, nor how many weddings I have performed. Most weddings are ordinary, nothing unusual; but every so often there is a wedding that is just a little different—there is that something extra that sets it apart.

Whereas I do not remember the first funeral I conducted, performing my first wedding is well remembered. Had I been marrying the President of the United States, I could not have been more excited or proud.

One Friday, up at the little store here on the creek, we were all sitting around talking and laughing. One young man sat there but never entered into the conversation. When I started to leave he followed me to the car.

"Joe, I aim to get married tomorrow. Can you marry me?"

"Of course," I stammered. "What time will you be down?"

"Sometime before noon," he replied calmly.

Never in all of my life had I known such excitement! The

marriage service in the *Book of Common Worship* was studied that night for a long, long time, and before going to bed I practically knew the entire service word for word.

What an awesome responsibility! I had the power to perform marriages; to unite two persons into one! Of course, all of this was through the blessing of the Lord and the guidance of the Holy Spirit.

Early Saturday morning I went into Booneville, having decided that there was enough money to purchase two plates, two cups and saucers, and two glasses. This would be my gift to the bride and groom.

At 10:30 a.m., the wedding party—the young man and his bride-to-be, plus the two required witnesses—walked up the hill to the manse, their faces beaming with joy.

The day of performing my first wedding had arrived and much pomp and majesty were poured forth in my new ministerial voice:

"Wilt thou have this Man to be thy husband, and wilt thou pledge thy troth to him, in all love and honor, in all duty and service, in all faith and tenderness, to live with him, and cherish him, according to the ordinance of God, in the holy bond of marriage?"

She paused. "I reckon I do," was her solemn reply.

The marriage license had been placed on a table by the door and, during the ceremony the wind blew the license outside. After repeating the necessary questions to the prospective groom, and accepting his eager reply, "I sure do," I pronounced them husband and wife. After he had kissed his bride, we all went outside to look for the license. In time it was found over the hill by the creek.

Since they had no transportation, after the service I drove them to the hollow in which they would be living. As they got out of the car, I handed the man the small package which had been prepared for them.

He smiled. "We sure do thank you, Joe. We thank you a lot."

The young bride, who had lived on the other side of Booneville, brought two pillowcases filled with clothes as her dowry.

Proudly, the man started walking up the hollow. Following a few steps behind, with the pillowcases and the small package clutched tightly within her arms, the young girl followed obediently.

At the bend of the road, he stopped—evidently thinking they could no longer be seen—took the package and pillowcases in one arm and tenderly placed the other arm around his new wife.

They had so little of the material blessings with which most couples begin a marriage; and yet, they possessed the greatest blessing of all—an abundance of love!

I don't know who was happier that day, the couple who had just been married, or the young minister who had just performed his first marriage ceremony!

Another wedding I performed was to haunt me for a long, long time.

She was a beautiful girl; a person of great talent; graduated from one of our better colleges, and we all loved her deeply. She was sweet, kind, and gentle and every one admired her striking beauty.

The ceremony was a simple one, in the home, with a few relatives and close friends.

When the time came for repeating the vows, she hesitated —then stopped. Her lips were trembling, and I silently prayed that she could continue.

Being from a prominent family, the story of her life was

well-known. Her parents were leaders in their church and deeply religious, never missing a Sunday and working very hard within the congregation. At one time she had been very much in love with an extremely handsome boy who was not of the church. In fact, he was not anywhere *close* to the church; but they were inseparable, and very much in love. Everyone presumed that they would eventually marry. He, too, was quite a remarkable person, filled with gaiety and the joy of life. Wherever he was there was always laughter. People liked him immensely. There was one problem. He drank and her parents strongly disapproved of the boy; so, quite suddenly, the romance ended.

In time she found someone else. This time the boy was a respected member of the church who met the approval of her parents, and after a brief courtship the date was set for their wedding.

The pause in the service took a few seconds, but it seemed more like an hour. Finally, with an almost inaudible voice she pronounced the boy's name and completed the vow.

After the wedding there were congratulations and best wishes, but I noticed tears within her eyes. She seemed to be looking far away, beyond the present moment to a time once filled with laughter, to days never to be possible again.

Through the years, most of my weddings were on the spur of the moment with no prior knowledge that they were to take place. A couple would simply drive up on the hill with marriage license in hand; or else they called and were at the manse within a few minutes. Very few weddings were church weddings.

In seminary, we were taught always to counsel the couple prior to a wedding.

Without prior notice one couple drove up to the manse and asked to be married. Being new in the ministry I decided that it was time to practice my ministerial obligations; so, feeling the need to counsel—and wanting to counsel, and realizing that it was my duty to counsel—I began to talk with the couple. Were they ready for the responsibilities of marriage? Did they understand the sacredness of marriage? I spoke for about thirty minutes, resplendent in all my theological training. Everyone was bored and the young man's eyes remained constantly on his watch.

Then I read the marriage license. The girl was only *thirteen* years of age. Thirteen? I exploded. Getting married at thirteen—there were laws prohibiting marriage at such an early age.

This was far more serious than I had thought; so, again I cautioned them about the responsibilities of marriage, the sacredness of marriage, and the seriousness of marriage.

"You gonna marry us or not?" the young man asked.

Thirteen years old! I was in shock!

Finally, in desperation I turned to the young girl and asked, "What would your mother say? What would your mother think? Thirteen years old and getting married!"

The young woman with her jumped to her feet and shouted angrily, "I'm her mother. *Marry her!*"

That was my first—but not to be my last—shotgun wedding.

One morning bright and early, an old car came up on the hill, and a young girl came running up to the front door of the manse.

"How much do you charge for a wedding?" she asked nervously.

"Nothing," I replied cheerfully. "It has always been my gift to the bride and groom."

She smiled in disbelief, then rushed back to the car, returning with a young boy and two witnesses.

She had no new wedding dress, and her shoes were pitiful and worn. The coat was much too thin for the cold winter air; however, she was happy and there was a glowing radiance upon her young face that I never will forget.

After the ceremony she tried to press a wadded-up dollar bill into my hand but I refused.

As their old car drove off the hill, she reached through a broken window and waved good-bye.

I am sure the Queen of England could not have been any happier at her wedding.

All of my weddings were not for the young; far from it. Nor were all of my weddings for Presbyterians. I married the wealthy, the poor, the learned, the unlearned, the fat and the lean, the old and the young, and Presbyterian and non-Presbyterian.

An elderly couple once stood before me to get married (he was seventy-eight and she was seventy-six), and they could not keep their hands off each other.

They finally joined hands and I read the vows: "And I do promise and covenant."

The old man paused, unsure that he could remember the exact words. I emphasized "covenant" slowly. He winked at me, and in a loud voice proclaimed, "And I do promise and, uh, covenant. Praise the Lord! Yes, praise the Lord. Hallelujah."

I continued: "Before God and these witnesses."

He kissed the woman passionately, then faced me.

"Would you repeat that, please."

"Before God and these witnesses."

He winked again. "Preacher, I ain't never been so happy in all my life. Praise the Lord! Before God and these witnesses —if you say so!"

I read on, a little worried at the events as they progressed: "To be thy loving and faithful husband."

He smiled again. He really liked that line. Turning again to the woman, he hugged her, picked her up in his arms and swung her around. "Honey, you've got you a man now. The preacher just read, and I happily repeat, TO BE THY LOVING AND FAITHFUL HUSBAND. Praise the Lord. Ain't life grand? I am gonna love you all I can."

The service continued solemnly: "In plenty and in want."

"Honey, you ain't going to want while I'm around."

I looked up. Our eyes met and I said softly, "You must repeat the line I just read."

"Repeat it again if you don't mind." He seemed amused.

"In plenty and in want."

"In plenty and in want. Praise the Lord. Hallelujah, Baby Jesus. If I was any happier, I would just fly away."

In due time they were married and quickly departed. I took two aspirin and went to bed.

There were many beautiful and expensive weddings at both the Cow Creek and the little Indian Creek Churches. Beautiful gowns were made with love and care; tuxedos in various colors were rented, either from Lexington or Jackson; large artistic arrangements of flowers; bridesmaids, attendants, flower girls and ring bearers all became a part of the wedding scene. And the reception was usually held in the back room of the church or, at Indian Creek, in the sanctuary. But the weddings I remember are the ones that were different.

One wedding was a nightmare. A schoolteacher—a perfectionist—everything had to be exactly right. Not ninety-four percent right, but one hundred percent right. Pictures were taken down, choir robes placed out of sight. Over and

The "Jeep for Joe" and kids.

over again, we rehearsed the ceremony. Her husband-to-be was a quiet man by the name of Horace. I lived in constant fear that during the service I, being nervous, would pronounce the intended groom's name as Horse. Horse—heaven forbid! Would she take "Horse" to be her wedded husband?

I still give thanks today that, in that nightmarish wedding of perfection, there were no errors, no blunders, no mistakes, and that I did not say "Horse" instead of Horace.

Weddings can be so unpredictable.

On one occasion, at a beautiful church wedding, I looked down at the bride's bouquet and the stems—like antennae—were quivering uncontrollably. I never saw anyone so nervous, and it was rather difficult to suppress my laughter.

On another occasion I looked down and noticed that the bride, who wore a *white* wedding gown, was six months pregnant!

And there was the time when the husband-to-be was so drunk he could barely stand. My first impulse was to stop the wedding, feeling that perhaps it was sacrilegious to perform a ceremony under such conditions; but, I reconsidered and the wedding went on.

How can I ever forget the wedding where the bride, who laughed so easily, started laughing and couldn't stop. Right in the middle of the ceremony she started laughing. I paused. We all had a good laugh and, after a few minutes, the wedding ceremony continued.

The bride-to-be was from Ohio, and her family wanted only the best; so money was no problem. Tuxedos were rented and the church was beautifully decorated with expensive floral arrangements. Food was catered to the home afterwards. Surely it was one of the most elaborate weddings ever in the Cow Creek Church.

The boy was from Indian Creek, and I doubt seriously if he had ever attended a church wedding before. This certainly was a new experience; quite different from hunting and fishing.

Everything went well until the end. "Please kneel for the benediction," I said, softly.

It was then that I noticed that he was about to go down. His eyes closed. Slowly his knees buckled. Quickly I reached out, catching him just before he hit the floor. This was to be my only wedding wherein someone fainted.

The most beautiful wedding I ever performed was in the little Indian Creek Presbyterian Church, when Susie Marshall married McKinley Bowling.

Lela Thomas and several of the girls had gone to the woods and collected moss, which they made into an altar. With wild flowers from the hills, Lela artistically decorated the little church. It was done with taste and simplicity. Yet, there was a grandeur and beauty that I had never seen before —nor since. A simple wedding, a handsome couple, and wild flowers from the hills occasioned my most beautiful wedding.

They had been to the manse several times to get married, and on each occasion I had not been there. Since I had no telephone at the time the only way to contact me was to come to the manse. But, alas, Joe Powlas could not be found and they wanted desperately to get married.

One day I went up the creek to our little country store and was surprised when a boy and girl started running toward me. "Grab him," the girl yelled. "Don't let him get away."

He was six feet tall, and he held me—*securely.*

"You have the license, don't you?" she asked the boy.

"Sure do," he replied.

"Then let's get married *now,* while we can!"

Quickly, they grabbed two witnesses and we all went back to the manse.

Only then did she realize that she was barefooted and still had on overalls. Hanging at home was a beautiful new wedding dress, made especially for the occasion; but there was no time for getting ready now.

So I performed my one and only wedding where the bride was barefooted—and in overall pants. She was beautiful; far more attractive than the average mountain girl, and her face beamed with happiness.

As I signed the wedding forms she turned to me and whispered, "If you ever tell *anyone* that I got married barefooted," she paused and smiled, "I'll kill you."

One wedding certainly left an indelible mark upon my life and brought tears to my eyes.

The marriage vows were spoken out in the yard, out under a large maple tree. Nearby, there were plows, several hound dogs, and a chicken coup, but the grounds were immaculately clean.

Prior to the wedding march, Johnny Cash—via an old record player which had been strategically placed in the yard —sang several love songs. One of the songs was "I Walk the Line," but I cannot remember the others.

A brother, perhaps fifteen years of age, clad in overalls, sat on the porch and played the guitar. As the couple joined hands and walked across the yard, he majestically strummed on the guitar "Here Comes the Bride." Never before in my life had I ever heard the wedding march played on a guitar!

Following the ceremony I lingered awhile, drank Kool-Aid, and ate cookies and dried-apple stack cake. What a beautiful service. Even the hound dogs looked happy.

Billy Bruce lived at the mouth of Cow Creek, about four

miles below the manse, and he courted a girl up the hollow on Beech Fork, about a mile above the manse. Since he had no means of transportation, he walked, and since his dates sometimes lasted until two o'clock in the morning, he would often knock on my front door during the early morning hours with the same question. "It's me, Joe. Do you mind if I come in and spend the night on your couch? It's a long way back home at this time of night."

This happened so often that the front door automatically would be left unlocked and, sometimes during the night or the early morning Billy Bruce would come in and bed down for the night.

Rarely has one seen such love. He literally worshipped Lucy. She was constantly in his mind, his thoughts, and in his speech.

One morning, after several years of courtship, he left the manse quietly, in deep silence, and I was fearful that they may have had a quarrel. In a few minutes he walked back into the manse. There was only silence.

I asked. "Billy Bruce, is something wrong?"

He hesitated. "Yes, Joe, there is."

"Can I help you?"

Again he hesitated. "Yes, Joe, you can, but I am afraid to ask, afraid that you might think me too forward."

Black headed, strong, always joyful, I simply could not imagine how Billy Bruce could have any great problems.

I smiled, "Go ahead and ask me. It's worth a try."

He turned and looked up toward the church, then down toward the creek. "You know Lucy and I are getting married before too long." He spoke softly, almost in a whisper. "Her folks . . . well, her folks . . . there are a lot in her family. And you know that there are a lot in my family . . . and . . . He paused for a few seconds. ". . . and I just don't have the money to go to a motel for our first night." He paused in embarrassment. "Could we spend our wedding night here at the manse?"

Then I understood.

For weeks Billy Bruce and I cleaned and polished the old building in preparation for the special event, and, in time, the wedding day arrived. Upstairs over my bedroom door I placed a hand-painted sign, *"Bridal Suite"* and made sure there was plenty of food downstairs in the refrigerator.

After the brief ceremony, I congratulated and conveyed my best wishes to Bill and Lucy; then waved good-bye, got in my car and headed up the creek to spend the night at the home of Earl.

Although weddings are sacred and serious, there are occasions when one simply has to laugh. Although I tried, on different occasions, to retain my composure, nothing—absolutely nothing—could keep me from breaking out in laughter or with a smile.

The home was crowded with people from the creek and at eleven o'clock, the appointed time, I took my place in front of the couple and started reading from the *Book of Common Worship:*

"Dearly beloved, we are assembled here in the presence of God to join this Man and this Woman in holy marriage; which is instituted of God, regulated . . ."

Directly behind and above my head, a bird emerged from the cuckoo clock and cuck-ooed eleven times! Startled and embarrassed, and unable to contain my laughter, it took me fully two minutes before I could continue.

The incident brought back memories of a visit I once made to the Lewinsville Presbyterian Church, in McLean, Virginia. After a speaking engagement before the Women's Association, I was taken to the home of one of the members, where I would spend the night; and, early the next morning, he would take me to the airport for my flight back to Lexington. My host, an officer in the army, had spent several years in Germany, and one of the mementos he had brought back was a large cuckoo clock which had been placed just outside my bedroom door. Tired and eager for sleep, I soon discovered that there would be no sleeping that night, for every hour the cuckoo bird emerged and cuck-ooed the hour; and every quarter hour the stupid thing cuck-ooed again. I never slept a wink the entire night.

The next morning, en route to the airport, my host asked how I had rested during the night. Politely, I assured him that I had slept rather well, silently whispering a prayer, asking forgiveness for my untruthfulness.

On the flight back to Kentucky, I closed my eyes and *tried* to sleep, but all all that could be heard above the noise of the jet engines was a continuous cuck-oo, cuck-oo, cuck-oo.

3

He was small for his age, but he stood quite tall that morning at the front door of the manse. Although the ground was frozen and snowflakes were falling gently to the ground, he had walked barefooted across the hill. "Joe, do you have any shoes I might borrow?" he asked quietly.

Through the years used clothing had become a vital part of our ministry. From the Board of National Missions in New York we received support from interested outside churches. Clothing, layettes, and Christmas gifts were shared and we —the Presbyterian Church—became known as a church that cared.

At Christmas time the gifts were always given away. There was never any charge for any gift, but we *sold* our used clothing. My philosophy was that "charity undermined self-respect." The ability to pay retained that element of self-respect that was so important to mountain people. If one was unable to pay in money, the amount due could always be paid in eggs, potatoes, labor, etc. One man even paid for a layette with blackberries.

Of course there were exceptions to every rule. If a fire occurred, and a home was destroyed, as a church we always sought to help, giving free clothing, blankets and kitchen utensils.

At Cow Creek the clothing was sold at clothing auctions.

Lucy, Lois, and Verne worked with the clothing, sorting and getting it ready for the sales. At Booneville, and at Indian Creek, each item was sold for five cents. In the Booneville Church, Circle Five took charge of the monthly sales which were held the first Wednesday of every month.

The money received for the clothing was used for many purposes: postage, office supplies, youth work, gasoline for the church van, and labor. Part of my salary also came from the clothing sales. At times, clothing money was used to help pay for other large projects: a piano for the Cow Creek manse, a public address system for the church, the church van, and the construction of the Indian Creek Church.

The women loved the clothing sales, and the sales became a vital part of our ministry. It also became a major social event for the women of the creek—as well as a supplement for the clothes closets of the homes. In time, the clothing center at Cow Creek became known to some as "THE POWLAS MALL."

In the early days I conducted the clothing sales alone. There was a lot of enjoyment and excitement. We all eagerly looked forward to accumulating enough clothing so that word could go out that there was going to be a sale.

Forester Robinson would bring his pickup truck over to Cow Creek—in payment I extended him two dollars worth of credit—and haul the clothing back across the hill to the Indian Creek Church, where the crowd would already be gathered. We placed the clothing out on the benches and the people would browse, selecting and counting the articles they wanted. They knew exactly what they could buy for whatever amount of money they had to spend, and I would be paid five cents per article.

Every so often there would be a bidding sale, where an article would be held up and the people would be asked to bid on it, with the highest bidder receiving the article.

There were two articles the women dearly loved—just two! Women's handkerchiefs and women's housecoats! These two items *always* brought the highest prices. To this day I have often wondered why! It did not matter if they were faded, worn, or ragged, these two items always brought top prices.

There were many who did not agree that the clothing should be sold; and once, a minister of another denomination stood on the front porch of the Cow Creek manse and stormily denounced my policy of selling the clothing. "The clothing should be given away," he said. "You have no right to charge poor people."

In his own church he, too, had clothing sales, but his sales were quite different. First, only those of *his* denomination and *his* church were able to receive the clothing. Secondly, everything was free. Word came to me that there had been an awful fight in his church at one of the clothing sales. It seems that several ladies all wanted the same coat.

His ministry did not last long and, before leaving, he came back over to Cow Creek, stood in the identical place, and said, "Joe, you were right. Charity does undermine self-respect, and it also causes a lot of unnecessary trouble."

So, all of our clothing was sold, and through the years the boxes kept coming—big boxes, little boxes, long boxes and short boxes. We never knew what might be contained within! Every so often we would receive a set of false teeth. Quite often, one shoe—an excellent shoe—would be received without its mate. One woman from Pennsylvania continually sent us used tinfoil.

Most of the clothing we received—about ninety-five percent—was good, clean, and usable, but every so often a box would arrive that contained clothing that could not be used.

One day the call came from a lady who lived in Dayton, Ohio, asking us to bring our van because she had an attic full of clothing to give us. Overjoyed, we drove the two-hundred and twenty-four mile trip to Dayton. Since the lady worked, we could not pick up the clothing until after five-thirty p.m. She was sweet, kind, and gentle and had prepared a delicious supper of fried chicken for us. The boxes carefully had been stored in the attic, so we had to make trip after trip up and down two flights of stairs. Finally the van was filled, and after nine p.m. we headed back to Kentucky. The next morning all of the boxes had to be taken up the creek and burned. *Everything* was mildewed and rotten. *Not one piece—not one article—was usable.* We had driven four-hundred and forty-eight miles for a load of clothing that could not be used!

One day we were mystified to find within one of the boxes a small black object, about the size of two hands cupped together. Attached to the object was a long black cord. When we plugged it into an electrical outlet the little black object made a humming sound. It did not move. There were no vibrations. We searched through the Sears, Montgomery Ward, and Spiegel catalogs, but no one could determine what the item might be or what it was supposed to do. We never did find out its intended mission in life. It simply sat there quite peacefully and hummed, and it almost drove us crazy trying to find out what it was—or did! To this day we have no idea.

I remember so well the delightful couple who lived on Salisbury Avenue in Columbus, Ohio. Roger Strauss, a retired lawyer, and his wife, Ethel, came to Cow Creek at least once a year—sometimes twice—and their large Buick automobile was always loaded with clothing. A luncheon would be prepared at the manse. (My secret was that I used

Sweet Sue's delicious chicken and dumplings and Mrs. Smith's apple pie, both secured at the local Bestway Store in Booneville.) The menu was always the same, and how that man loved that chicken and dumplings!

Some weeks after one of her trips, a very excited Ethel Strauss called and informed me that Roger had inadvertently packed her beautiful green pantsuit in one of the boxes which they had brought down to Cow Creek. It was brand-new and had cost over two hundred dollars. She asked if we would go over to the Summer White House and go through the boxes *carefully* and see if the pantsuit could be found.

Sadly, I informed her that we had already had our clothing sale and that every item had been sold, but I promised her that I would make a special appeal from the pulpit the following Sunday. True to my word, I made the announcement in all three churchs: We desperately needed a green pantsuit that had been sent down to Cow Creek by error. Would the purchaser of this item please return it and his money would be refunded.

We never heard a word about the two-hundred dollar green pantsuit. It had been sold for a nickel and, in all probability, bought by a Baptist.

We were always grateful for used clothing. During the latter years of my ministry a supplement to my salary came through the sale of the clothing, so I personally welcomed and cherished each and every box. But there was one box that was to give me a special lift at a much needed time.

Word had come that one of our Elders had suffered a heart attack; so, I immediately jumped into my car and hurried to Central Baptist Hospital in Lexington. He was a dear soul; so kind, so humble, so beloved by our congregation; so it was imperative that the trip be made as quickly as possible.

Lexington was about ninety-two miles away, and all the

way there my one prayer was that I might reach him in time.

Excited and in a hurry, I tore my pants on the side of the door while getting out of the car in the hospital parking lot. In fact, my entire rear-end was ripped out. What a dilemma! I was not wearing a suit, so there was no coat to cover my bottom. I had only six dollars in my billfold, certainly not enough to purchase a pair of pants. The Shell credit card was of no consolation, since it was impossible to buy clothing with a gasoline credit card, but I had come too far, now, not to see the Elder. Quickly I bowed my head and prayed, and for once I prayed for a miracle! Anything, Lord. Anything!

Then I saw it—a box on the back seat of the car. A box of clothing had arrived that morning and I had placed it in the car. Lord, please don't let it be women's clothing. Please, Lord—and I don't mean to be sacrilegious—please, Lord, let there be a pair of men's pants. It doesn't really matter if they don't fit exactly. Lord—please—just let there be a pair of pants!

Quickly, and with faith, the box was opened.

There were no pants! Only a large black, woolly, overcoat. I don't know what the material was—just black, woolly, fuzzy material.

It was the latter part of August, and the temperature that day was well over one hundred degrees; but I got out of the car, put on the large, black, fuzzy overcoat, which adequately covered my torn bottom, and marched triumphantly toward the hospital.

People stopped and stared as I walked by. Little children pointed in my direction and laughed. I am sure that everyone was wondering why a grown man would be wearing an overcoat on such a hot day.

The receptionist was just as bemused and bewildered as she informed me that our Elder had been placed in the Intensive Care Unit.

66

Normally, in a hospital a minister is allowed to visit an ill church member at any time, but I was being refused permission to do so.

I protested and tried to explain my situation, but the head nurse adamantly stated that I could not enter.

"But I *am* a Presbyterian minister," I insisted.

The lady in white looked me up and down and asked in total disbelief, *"You,* a Presbyterian minister?"

"Yes, a Presbyterian minister," was my calm reply. So, with the big black coat on, I was admitted to the Intensive Care Unit. While I stood by his side, the Elder looked up, smiled, and thanked me for coming. After a brief prayer I left the hospital.

As I walked across the parking lot to the car, I was so grateful for the box that had arrived that day. Through its coming, the opportunity had been given to me to visit with the elder who was to live for only a short time longer.

We needed and appreciated the used clothing. It was a blessing to the people of our area, and it became a blessing, financially, in our ministry, paying for many activities and items which otherwise would not have been possible.

From time to time newsletters were sent out to those who shared in our work. We started with just one name in our "Little Green Box," but, in time, the list of interested individuals and churches grew to over eleven hundred. Most of our support came from Ohio and Pennsylvania, but the list included individuals from most of the fifty states.

A brief newsletter, sharing our work, was sent out two or three times a year but in the early years, feeling that it was of little or no interest, this was discontinued. Then a letter came all the way from Africa, the sender (who was a missionary to whom our letters had been forwarded by a mother in Pittsburgh), stated that she missed the letters and to please continue sending them out. So, the word of our work started flowing again.

One such newsletter became quite a hit with many Women's Associations, and it was rewarding to learn that the letter, written in dialog, was given by the ladies in churches in Ohio, New York, Pennsylvania and Indiana. Once, while in Columbus, Ohio, before my speaking engagement, the president of the Women's Association said: "Joe, we have a surprise for you."

The lights went out, the curtain was drawn, and there on the stage were several ladies giving a presentation of my newsletter. Never had I been so honored!

St. Peter:	I hear that down on earth there is a little bit of heaven called Cow Creek.
Chorus:	There is! There is!
St. Peter:	I believe that we have a man there by the name of Joe—Joe Powlas.
Chorus:	That's right! That's right!
St. Peter:	I wonder what is going on down there. We have not had a monthly report from that man now for *(turning aside)*—Brother Ben, would you please check the books.
Brother Ben:	Not since June, St. Peter. Not since last June.
Chorus:	Ah! Ah! Ah! *(remorsefully)*
St. Peter:	*(rubbing chin)* Not since last June! I wonder what on earth is going on down there. St. Agnes, I appoint you and Sister Bessie and Brother Robert—yes, Sister Martha, you can go, also. I appoint you all to go down there as a special committee and see what Brother Powlas is doing. And I want a WRITTEN report.
Sister Bessie:	Can I take Sister Suzy along, too? She's just

dying to see the manse since the renovation. You know—a new furnace, new bathrooms, new floors, and . . .

St. Peter: No, Sister Bessie, I cannot grant your request. Sister Suzy talks a little too much and I am a'feared she'd only tarry your mission.

(Conversation is interrupted by the blowing of trumpets.)

St. Peter: Just a minute. Someone is knocking at the gate.

Old Man: Howdy. Are you *(pauses)* St. Peter?

St. Peter: *(proudly, extending hand)* I am, and who might you be?

Old Man: *(just as proud)* I am Clem McIntosh, from Crooked Hollow, near the Left Hand Fork of Cow Creek, Owsley County, Kentucky.

Chorus: Did you say "Cow Creek?"

Old Man: Yep, Cow Creek. Cow Creek, Kentucky.

St. Peter: Come closer, Clemus Daniel McIntosh *(reading from book)*, son of Albert and Metilda McIntosh.

Old Man: *(frightened)* Your honor, I've been a pretty good man. Now, I know that there are a few things I hate to reckon to—like the time . . .

St. Peter: Now, don't get worried. I've already let you in the gate. We are all just dying to know what is happening down on Cow Creek. You know Joe Powlas, I guess?

Old Man: Yep, sure do. *(relieved)* Well, a lot has been going on down there. You might say that it was a really good year. First of all, there were a lot of visitors and youth groups. They came from Pennsylvania, Ohio, Virginia, New York, Tennessee, Indiana and North Carolina. Sorta funny—one night they had seventy-one persons there and there just wasn't enough room for everyone to bed down. Finally, about eleven-thirty that night, they had it all settled. Some were bedded down in the manse, some in the Summer White House, some in the back of the church, and some took sleeping bags and spent the night in the cemetery behind the church.

Chorus: Wonderful place to rest! Wonderful place to rest!

Sister Suzy: Pardon the interruption, Brother Clem, but didn't something wonderful happen about the middle of the summer?

Old Man: *(scratching a head of white hair)* You are right, Sister Suzy. A group of young people from the Lewinsville Presbyterian Church, in McLean, Virginia, who for several summers had collected TV books—that's sorta like Sunday school books with little green stamps in them—well, they collected enough to present to the Cow Creek Church a beautiful new Ford Club Wagon. It can transport ten ladies to their weekly quilting, or fifteen children to their youth meetings and, of course, it is used on Sunday mornings for transportation. Then—*(pauses, excited)* and then the church invited Brother Joe and eleven Senior-Hi's to come to their church in Virginia and visit with them and see Washington, D.C.

Sister Bessie: Sure is a wonderful story, Brother Clem. Go on.

Old Man: Thank you, Sister Bessie. Well, it was just

about the most exciting thing that ever happened—the new church van and the trip to Washington, D.C.—and everyone is still talking about it. Folks sure are good, aren't they?

Chorus: They are! They are!

Old Man: And for Vacation Bible School, a wonderful group of folks came down. Dale and Melina Campbell, Mildred McMahon, Wiley and Louise Stiles. The young folks from Washington, Pennsylvania, came down and conducted the Bible School at Cow Creek, and the McLean Group had Vacation Bible School over at Indian Creek.

Sister Martha: Listen, girls, this sounds great. St. Peter, I personally volunteer right here and now to go down next summer and help out with Vacation Bible School at Cow Creek.

St. Peter: That's awfully kind of you, Sister Martha, but kindly remember that you have already passed on to your reward.

Sister Suzy: Didn't something else wonderful happen? The sister from Pennsylvania was telling me about it.

Old Man: You're right, Sister Suzy. Lew and Peg Hays (he is commissioner of Pony and Colt baseball) came down and spent Thanksgiving at the manse.

Sister Suzy: Just what does our brother Joe do, Brother Clem?

Old Man: Well, I don't rightly know. He's got one foot in heaven, but I'm not quite sure where the other one is 'cause he seems to do a lot of coming and going. He drives two thousand

| | miles each month; preaches twice on Sunday —at the Cow Creek Church and the Indian Creek Church—teaches the adult Sunday school class on Sunday morning; has two youth meetings a week; two women's meetings a week; conducts choir practice each Thursday night; he visits the sick; marries the young—and the old; buries the dead, and just a lot of things. |

St. Peter: I hate to interrupt this gathering folks, but it is time for our afternoon sing. Let us all go down by the river.

Sister Martha: Tell me, Brother Clem, is our brother Joe happy down there?

Old Man: Yes, he's awfully happy. Just real happy.

St. Peter: Come, folks, down to the river side.

Sister Martha: I hear that Christmas on Cow Creek is a most joyous event.

St. Peter: You are tarrying, good people.

Old Man: Yes, it is a beautiful experience. But, I'll have to tell you about that at a later time.

Sister Martha: Is Cow Creek really that beautiful—as beautiful as heaven—Brother Clem?

Old Man: *(pauses)* It ain't the *place* exactly. I guess it's just the folks who live there.

One newsletter went out that caused quite a sensation and numerous letters came back.

THE LETTER THAT CAME TODAY

"Your first letter came many, many years ago. Through the Board of National Missions in New York you had learned about our ministry and your letter was filled with questions. And then, shortly after I answered, the boxes began to arrive. Usually, it was children's clothing—always clean and ironed, but every so often there would be dresses, men's clothing and household articles. Then, at Christmas, there would be a box of toys. The box was never large, but it always came.

"Occasionally, you would write about your church and the activities of the Women's Association. Just little bits of news that made your letters so informative and interesting. Through the years, with your Bake Sales, Talent Shows and Quilting Bees, you and your church were part of our growth. You were instrumental in our securing chairs for the manse when we had but three or four—and lastly, you helped us make the down payment on our much-needed new church van (the second of three vans).

"One summer you and your husband went to Europe and the postcards came back from Switzerland, England, France and Italy. How I appreciated the remembrance! Then, when you returned home, you sent snapshots, and on the back of each picture you thoughtfully shared the occasion with us.

"Your husband passed away unexpectedly, and from your letters I knew of your grief, your sorrow, and your loneliness. Following his death you became more active in your church and in your Association projects. Your letters once again reflected your great Christian spirit and concern. In your letter, received not too long ago, you spoke again of your desire to visit Cow Creek. This time you stated that the dream would become a reality because, before too long, some friends would drive you down. While not staying more than a day, you would have the opportunity to be with us; have lunch here at the manse; see the churches, and to meet our people. I rejoiced at this news.

"A few minutes ago I returned from the post office. In my hand I hold the letter I mailed to you two weeks ago. It has been returned stamped, DECEASED—Return to Sender.

"I never had the honor of meeting you; talking with you; or knowing you but you cannot know the sadness I feel as I now hold the letter in my hand. Through the years you have been a wonderful, wonderful friend and I will miss you—more than you can ever know."

The letter referred to a lady from the state of Michigan, but after the newsletter was sent out, sixteen letters came back, each informing me that the sender was not dead, but that she was very much alive. Since no names had been mentioned, evidentially there were many widows who had identified themselves with the dear lady from Michigan.

Through the years no church supported our ministry as did the Westminster Presbyterian Church of Akron, Ohio. Each May an eighteen-wheeler came to Cow Creek, loaded with all kinds of good things. The question each year during early Spring was, "Will the truck come again?" It always did, bringing "ohs" and "ahs" and "Look at that!" and "How pretty!"

Although we received clothing throughout the course of the year from other sources, Westminster was the only church that sent refrigerators, stoves, pots and pans, beds, sofas, typewriters, and washers and dryers in addition to the clothing. One could not imagine the joy and anticipation of wondering just what would be sent each year. As one little girl so aptly stated during a youth session concerning happiness, peace and joy: *"Happiness is the eighteen-wheeler that comes from Akron!"*

In Winchester there is a religious bookstore called the Bethany Book Room. Often, when going to Lexington, a stop would be made for supplies—whether it be certificates, hymnals, or study books. Each visit gave me the opportunity to see the painting *On the Road to Emmaus* and these few minutes kindled my desire to buy the picture; but, financially, this was impossible. More than anything else I wanted that painting but I knew that, in all probability, that dream would never come true.

One day a delightful couple from Indiana brought down a truckload of clothing. With the clothing there were several pictures, and one was the much-wanted *On the Road to Emmaus.* They were surprised at my joy! So, I told them of my long desire for the painting. They both laughed.

It seems that the picture had been hanging in the pastor's study. When the room was refurnished they decided to throw the painting away, so it was tossed outside in the trash can. The janitor, finding the picture, simply returned it to the Sunday School department. The Sunday School department, after carefully surveying their wallspace, decided they had no room for it. This time it was sent to a charitable organization within the city, along with several boxes of clothing. The charitable organization wanted the clothing, but *no* pictures! So, once again, it was returned to the church.

In desperation the minister proclaimed, "Let's send it to Joe Powlas, down at Cow Creek."

So, at long last, I was the recipient of the beautiful painting, *On the Road to Emmaus,* and immediately it was placed with love and affection on the wall of my study.

So, used clothing became a vital part of our ministry and, as we hauled boxes and boxes of clothing from church to church, we well remembered: "I was naked and you clothed me," and it was good to know that our labors were a blessing to those in need.

4

I look back now, remembering so well the little schoolhouse across the ravine where the children walked each day to school. There were two rooms and, at one time, both rooms were used, but when I came to Cow Creek the children studied in the lower room only.

One could stand on the porch of the old manse and hear the laughter of the children as they played "Round Town," and one could see the numerous dogs which followed the children to school. These dogs waited obediently and patiently until dismissal so they could follow their young masters home.

One day I entered the schoolhouse and silently took a seat at the back of the room. Twenty-five or thirty students had gathered for the purpose of securing their education. The students were in deep study and the teacher, Mrs. Margaret McIntosh, was busy at the board writing an assignment. The pine-paneled room was characteristic of a county school. There was a picture of George Washington on the wall above the blackboard; a potbellied stove stood ready to give warmth for the chilly days of winter; in the corner was a small library; and a mural, proudly constructed by tiny hands, had been tacked to the side of the wall. In the back of the room the dinner pails had been neatly arranged on a table, and the coats hung on pegs from the wall.

All eyes were on the teacher and I, too, followed her story with devout interest. In those days, the schools were allowed to have devotions and I was in awe of the hour.

"The heavenly Father," Mrs. McIntosh paused, "starts with a 'C'?"

"Cares," the children answered in unison!

She continued. "At that time there was the . . . Who knows what the 'F of the P' is?"

The children were silent. No one volunteered an answer; but, then, the words came from Charles: "The Feast of the Passover!" he answered triumphantly.

"Right! That is correct, Charles." She was pleased.

"Now, who can tell me who the Roman governor was at that time?"

"Pilate." The answer came from Verne, to the far left.

A long white bench had been placed in front of the room and, when called upon, each class would walk to the front to give their recitations. (The girls often giggled and turned their toes inward, which immediately brought forth more giggles.)

An attractive woman, Mrs. McIntosh, a mother of three, lived on the creek and was considered to be one of the best teachers in Owsley County. One was fascinated by her patience as she devoted an allotted amount of time to each grade. The other grades during this period would either work in the little library at the side of the room or else study their lessons.

She took her position in front of the first grade. "This morning we are going to talk about objects." She smiled and all the children—seven in number—looked up and immediately the first grade was in session.

"Name something to eat."

All of the children answered "ice cream," except one little boy who cried out, "groundhog."

"Name something to ride."

"A car."

"A pony."

Each child took his turn in giving an answer.

"A bicycle."

The last little boy, probably the one who had answered "groundhog," simply said, "Grandpa."

"Grandpa?" Mrs. McIntosh looked puzzled.

"Yep! Every night he gives me a ride on his back. He gets down on the floor and I ride my grandpa!" There was an awful lot of love in that simple answer!

"Now, can each person spell the answer you gave?"

There was silence. After all, this was only the first grade.

"I can spell car," answered Jimmy.

"Can anyone spell bicycle?"

A little girl with black hair timidly said, "I can't remember a 'b' from a 'd.' "

The teacher went to the blackboard and drew a 'd.'

"A 'd' has a tummy."

Then she drew a 'b.'

"A 'b' has a tail like a bunny rabbit."

The lesson continued.

"Name something pretty."

Alma Ruth stuck up her hand. "I think that a dog is the prettiest thing in the world."

Jimmy answered, "I like mules, so I am going to say mule. Once you get to know him, a mule is real pretty."

Carold smiled, "I like snow."

"Can you spell snow?"

"No," she answered, laughing.

"S-n-o-w, repeat after me, slowly. S-n-o-w." All of the children repeated the letters.

"Now, name something that can fly."

The answers were varied: "Birds." "Airplanes." "Buzzards."

"Can you spell bird?"

Carol raised her hand and slowly spelled "b-i-r-d."

"Now, name something that shines."

"The sun," came from Jimmy.

"The moon," was given by Ronald.

"The stars," was the answer given by Claude.

"In spelling sun, I get mixed up with Sue," Jimmy said, laughing.

Mrs. McIntosh paused for a few seconds.

"Now, finally, name someone you love."

The answers came quickly, mostly names of their fathers, mothers, brothers or sisters, but Claude, looking past the windows and out into the fields where the men were working, spoke with childlike tenderness. "I am going to say Pa." Pa was his grandfather, an elderly man, kind, gentle and humble, who lived with Claude's family.

And the seven students sat on the long white bench, where they were to learn the wonders and the mysteries of the universe.

The plaid shirt, torn overalls, checked blouse, occasional giggle, muddy shoes, curled hair, white bench, dinner pails, numbered tin cups by the large bucket of water—these were all a part of the little county school which, in time, would disappear and never again would there be found the greatness of simplicity as we once knew it.

They continued their studies.

"Take away part of Carol's name and you have a car." This remark came from Jimmy.

"Now, in your books, turn to page sixty-four."

Immediately there was the turning of pages and everyone found the page except one little girl.

Claude looked at the teacher, then to the little girl sitting beside him.

"She won't ever find it, Miss McIntosh," he said slowly.

The teacher helped the little black-headed girl, in the worn boots, find the page.

The story from the *First Grade Reader* that morning was about a breakfast in a barn. What a strange story, I thought; but the children enjoyed the reading and, as they took turns, each child read well, indicating they had all prepared their lessons.

"Babies always like milk," Alma Ruth smiled.

"I don't like buttermilk," was the reply from Carol.

"Where do you get butter?" Mrs. McIntosh asked.

"From milk."

"From cows."

"And where do you get raisins?" she continued.

For a moment there was silence, then Claude gave his opinion. "From beans!"

So, the story about breakfast continued and the children sparkled with excitement.

"Now, who can tell me what they had for breakfast at the barn that morning? All right, Claude, you have your hand up."

"Miss McIntosh," he answered, "we have our strawberry plants all set out."

The little ones returned to their seats and the second grade came to the long white bench and they, in turn, gave their recitations.

The morning passed all too quickly. I enjoyed the warmth of the room, the kindness of the children who, seeing me present, would look my way and smile every so often. Each child was special. Each child attended the little white church, and each child was a part of our Five and One-Half Club.

In the years to come, someone made a study and the conclusion was that there were more college graduates from Cow Creek, Kentucky, than from any other place in the United States in proportion to population! And all because of two women who came to Cow Creek in 1910 and started the Athenia Academy.

Once a week the Five and One-Half Club walked down to the manse for two hours of fellowship. First, we studied the *Shorter Catechism* (Who made you?—God! What else did God make?—God made all things!), then there was an hour or more of running and playing. They played such games as Kick the Can, Flying Dutchman and Snatch the Bacon; but most of all they loved ghost stories. They were much too young for real scary tales; however, they all delighted in the Edgar Allen Poe stories, and in the hand-me-down tales. Always, after a special scary night, I had to walk each child up each hollow after dark, for they were always too afraid to walk home alone.

A boy from Indian Creek walked over to the manse to play with the kids one afternoon. He arrived early, so he and I devised a little prank. When the kids arrived we would have a seance and, at the appropriate time, this boy, who would be hidden at the top of the stairs, would suddenly come running down. It seemed like a perfect plan, but actually it worked too well.

There were five kids present. We completed our study of the *Shorter Catechism,* and the kids learned the answers to five questions. Then we went outside and played some games; but, as it grew darker, they all wanted to go inside the manse and tell ghost stories. Everything was falling right into place—my master plan!

I sat in the middle of the floor on the hand-hooked rug

that Gertie Turner had made for the manse, and the children sat around me in a circle.

"Tonight," I smiled, "we are going to have a seance."

They all seemed puzzled. "Just what is a seance?" Alpha asked.

"A seance is where people still living talk with the dead!"

Immediately they all agreed that by all means we must have a seance!

"Who do you want to talk with?" I asked.

The children were so young that this created a problem; for, actually, there was no one within their remembrance that could be associated with death. But in the new cemetery which had just been started behind the church there was one fresh grave. Alpha immediately thought about that grave.

"Let's talk with Sam McIntosh," she said.

That was a perfect idea, so I continued. "Now, we have to have complete silence. No one can make a sound." For several minutes there was complete silence.

"Oh, I forgot one thing. We must turn out all the lights." There were some groans and some sighs as I turned out the one light in the living room. We were now in total darkness.

All the kids immediately drew closer to me, and to one another. For several minutes there was a ghostly silence, which I broke by asking the question, "What do we want to ask Sam?"

No one spoke until Charles timidly said, "Let's ask him if he went to heaven!"

So, in a slow, deep voice, I asked, "Did . . . you . . . go . . . to . . . heaven?"

The boy from Indian Creek, who had hidden and waited patiently at the head of the stairs, shouted from the top of the stairs, "HELL NO!" then came noisily running and stumbling down the stairs.

Pandemonium broke loose. Kids were jumping, arms

were flying and voices were screaming! Simultaneously, five children were scrambling and fighting, trying to sit in the lap of one minister, while ten arms tried desperately to find their way around his neck.

That had been on a Thursday night. Sunday morning, when Joe Powlas climbed into the Cow Creek pulpit, there were numerous scratches on his face and neck. One eye was black and he walked with a slow, painful limp.

Those kids are all grown now, and each has gone his own way: Charles is married and lives in Yadkinville, North Carolina; Carol has her doctorate, and now teaches at Eastern State University, at Richmond; Claude is an electrician and works in Lexington; Verne is in the insurance business in Corbin, and Alma Ruth teaches school in Estill County.

Though they are grown and successful and now have children of their own, to me they will *always* be the Five and One-Half Club of Cow Creek, Kentucky.

5

He was my best friend and I became acquainted with him at Crossnore, a D.A.R. School for Mountain Children down in western North Carolina. They called him "Roadman," because he had been born by the side of the road.

He died unexpectedly in the summer of 1939, and his last words were, "I know that I am going to die, but I will die *bravely.*" Everyone who knew him loved him, and he left an indelible mark upon those who had shared his friendship.

As a minister I was well-aware of needs unknown to other people; so, in his memory, The Roadman Fund was started. This fund, approved by the church, was to be used as the need arose, without my having to go through the Session. It was used to buy clothing and shoes; to share with a mother who remained at the bedside of her sick child in Lexington; to make our churches more attractive and beautiful; and it was used to pay those who were to become a part of our ministry at the three churches.

During my ministry, hospital calls were made each week on Wednesday, but if a member were critically ill the long trip to Lexington was made two or three times within the week.

Calls were made at Central Baptist, Good Samaritan, St. Joseph's, UK Medical Center, Humana, and the Veteran's Hospital. Other calls were made to hospitals in Manchester,

Richmond, Hazard and Irvine. Sometimes these calls were made at two or three o'clock in the morning.

It is important that a minister be by the bedside of those who are critically ill, and it is important that a minister be with the family of those who are ill as they wait, not knowing whether or not death is eminent. A minister's presence shows that he cares, and *this* is vitally important during a crisis.

Most of our people go to a hospital in Lexington. Occasionally the stay is longer than anticipated, and some are often confined to the hospital with little or no money. Always a mother will remain at the hospital with her child, refusing to leave until the child is completely out of danger. Although it may mean sleeping in a chair in the waiting room, she stays there, whether or not she has any money.

When I run into this kind of situation, I usually slip a twenty dollar bill—or even a fifty if it is available—into the mother's hand, always with the admonition, "Please, do not tell anyone about this. It will be *our* secret." The appreciation and the tears of joy are unbelievable.

On several occasions I have run into families visiting at the hospital who were from our county who did not even have gasoline money for the return trip home. They simply waited and prayed that someone would come along that they knew. I was grateful for our ministry during this hour of need.

From the Roadman Fund, toys would be bought for children who were fearful of impending surgery. Somehow, if they were clutching a talking doll or a teddy bear their pain always seemed to be so much lighter.

In all my years of ministry the Roadman Fund was never depleted. Even though it got quite low at times, a few dollars always remained in the account, and when a special need arose, somehow the money was always available.

Each year a financial statement was shared with the con-

James and Brackey Riley going fishing.

gregation so they would know exactly how the money had been spent.

So it was through a small boy down in North Carolina that a fund was created to spread, as best we could, the love and the beauty of God in the mountains of Kentucky.

In remembrance, there is a special place in my heart for the Crossnore School. We were always taught to work, to go to church, and to love and respect our country.

There were two hundred children in the dormitories. At the Little Boys' Dormitory, where Lynn Woody was the housefather, we had our nightly prayers, our snowball fights, the cold showers, and an abundance of love. He also taught us the meaning of *noblesse oblige.* I especially remember our Sunday night suppers of milk and cornbread. Nothing ever tasted as good!

As the years passed, I moved from the Little Boys' Dormitory to the Middle-Sized Boys' Dormitory, to the Big Boys' Dormitory. Along the way special friendships were established with Clarice and Ethel Burleson, Carl Lusk, Bobby Carswell, Cecil Greer and Gustie and Lockie Hollander. Each Saturday night there was square dancing in the D.A.R. dormitory. In the wintertime there was ice-skating on Dr. Sloop's dam (built to provide electricity for the community), and in the summer there were the hiking escapades to Haw Shaw and Grandfather Mountain, and sliding down Christmas Tree Hill with homemade sleds on the pine needles.

We were one family, united by a strong Presbyterian faith and held together—though materially poor—by a fellowship of love, compassion and concern.

During the course of the year different students, who were well-trained, went out to sing the mountain ballads and perform the folk dances before the supporting chapters of the

D.A.R. This might mean going to Raleigh, or Asheville, North Carolina, or to Knoxville, Tennessee.

One year an invitation came to Crossnore School to send a delegation of dancers and singers to Washington, D.C., to perform during the annual meeting of the D.A.R. Congress.

This invitation came during my senior year. Tall and lanky, without much voice and without much coordination, my one obsession was to go to Washington! I had never wanted anything so badly in my life. From the thirty or forty dancers available from our school, only twelve would be chosen.

My every thought, my every prayer, my every waking minute was obsessed with the determination that I was going to dance, *and* I was going to sing in Washington, D.C. Nothing else in my life had any significance nor any value.

So, for two months there was the intense preparation, the hard work. We practiced in the morning and we practiced after school. We sang the mountain ballads until at night I dreamed of nothing else.

Finally the day arrived. After supper Mrs. Sloop would discuss the trip in detail and then read the list of those selected.

She was as *big* in personality as she was *short* in stature, and she spoke with both love and authority.

All day I had prayed that I would be chosen. I prayed in the bathroom, I prayed during my classes, I prayed as we peeled potatoes that afternoon, and then, when I took my place at the supper table, I uttered one last desperate prayer.

"Please, God—I don't ask for much (except to get good grades), please—let my name be read tonight. Let Joe Powlas go to Washington to sing and dance. Please, God, please."

When Mrs. Sloop stood to speak, the dining room suddenly became as silent as a tomb. She recalled how she and the Doctor had been to Asheville. She told of eating at the S.

and W. Cafeteria, about a movie they had seen, and about some books she wanted us to read. She talked about the war, about the Soviet's capture of Odessa, about the Pacific Air Force hitting Truk Atoll, the massive Japanese naval fortress which guarded the Carolina Islands, and about how the Yanks and Nazis ceased firing for Easter Services.

She was an excellent speaker, always holding her audience spellbound, but would she never get to that list? My mind became tangled and I was angry.

Finally, with a smile, the words came: "Now, as most of you know, twelve of you have been chosen to go to Washington to the D.A.R. Congress to represent Crossnore School. This is a great honor and I know that those of you who have been chosen will represent our school well. I will now read the names of those who have been selected."

I could not breathe. Suddenly, it seemed that all the oxygen had left my body. Darkness closed in on me, but I was determined not to miss a single word. Mrs. Sloop began to read the list.

The names of the best and most talented individuals were read first. We all knew who those individuals were, but there were five borderline cases and my only chance was to be included in this category.

The final name was read.

The name "Joe Powlas" was *not* called.

Blindly, with tears in my eyes, I stumbled my way to the door, went out into the approaching darkness and found my way to Christmas Tree Hill, where, beneath the towering pine trees, I fell to the ground and cried as though my life were ending. Never had I known such sorrow and grief!

I stayed beneath the trees much too long. The two-hour study hall, which was mandatory each night, was closing as I slipped into the front door and climbed the stairs to my room. Through kindness and understanding, no one said a

word—not even Mr. Woodside who, as a strict discipli-
narian, had every right to ground me for two weeks for missing study hall.

So, my one and only chance to go to Washington, D.C.
while at Crossnore did not materialize, and I was to feel the
scars of this rejection for a long, long time.

Years later as I sat at the desk in the manse at Cow Creek,
the telephone rang.

"Joe," the voice said simply, "would you go to
Washington and speak at the Mayflower Hotel on behalf of
the D.A.R. schools in America?"

My trip to Washington had come at last—not as a singer
or dancer, but as a speaker, and I would not be representing
just one school but *all* of the D.A.R. approved schools in
America.

On an April 25th, in the ballroom of the Mayflower
Hotel, I stood and spoke, grateful for the opportunity of
sharing appreciation for the support and the help which these
ladies, through the years, had so generously shared with
homeless and underprivileged children. Their love and support gave a new home, a new start, to thousands of boys and
girls, including Joe Powlas and, in that hour, I was
thankful—so thankful—to have been a part of Crossnore
School.

I shared with them the fact that, during my school years,
I was the recipient of three D.A.R. medals and that this trust,
encouragement and recognition was to have a lasting effect
upon my life.

Also to have an effect upon my life was my third grade
school teacher, Miss Mamie Shirley; Elizabeth J. Nelson;
Margaret Collins; Dr. Eustus Sloop and Bobby Carswell—all
of whom I admired so greatly.

6

Christmas became the most wonderful time of the year at Cow Creek. No other event gave the happiness, joy and excitement as did our preparation of the Christmas bags. About a month prior to Christmas—around the last week in November—Christmas lists were compiled for the three churches. Boxes that had been sent by various churches and individuals during October and November were carefully opened, sorted, and the items counted. Little by little we readied for the task of preparing more than five hundred and fifty Christmas bags. We also packed additional boxes for families that were outside the church.

In the early days of my ministry Clyde Gabbard would help me and, since there were not too many bags to prepare at that time, the two of us worked perfectly together. I would write the name on the bag—Clyde would put in the fruit and the candy, then I would complete the bag by filling it with other available articles. We rarely talked! Earl McIntosh would also lend a helping hand from time to time.

As our ministry increased, and we went from one-hundred to two-hundred and then to over five-hundred bags, it became impossible for just two or three persons to do the work. Arvis Trosper and his two sons, Zackie and Junior, and Ricky Mazurek volunteered to help with the packing. Since we knew absolutely nothing about sizes,

Norm Thomas, Lela and Linda Bishop worked with the clothing, because they knew the correct size for each individual person. I did not know a size five from a size twenty in women's clothing. The sanctuary soon became the clothing distribution center.

Again, I kept the records, carefully writing the person's name on a bag and then checking the name from the list.

Arvis, Junior, Zackie and Ricky would place oranges, apples and candy in the bag, then add toys and school supplies. The women would then put in the clothing.

We never had enough for our teenagers, so a trip would always have to be made to Lexington to purchase at least one-hundred model cars to fill the bags for the boys, and additional items for the teen-age girls.

There seemed to be an abundance for the smaller children, but never enough for the older kids. Tucked into the adult bags were socks, ballpoint pens, gloves, aprons, towels, and occasionally a beautiful afghan that had been made by a group of women in Massachusetts and sent yearly by Florence Ryder. Most of the women in this group had arthritis so during the year they enjoyed knitting, as it gave them an opportunity to exercise their fingers. They would ship their beautiful handmade items to Cow Creek in October. Free shipping was provided by a freight company who delivered their cargo to the Second Presbyterian Church in Lexington where, with great joy, they were carefully placed in the back of my pickup truck and hauled to Cow Creek, ninety-two miles away.

For many of our children this gift from the church was to be their *only* remembrance. Christmas was the most wonderful of all occasions!

Strange that one should **remember** so vividly each and every Christmas!

The morning of December 25 was extremely cold. Shelby Moore and I climbed into the Jeep borrowed from Charles Long, in Booneville, and we made our way across frozen creeks and up rutted hollows. Since we had observed Holy Communion on Christmas Eve, we decided to deliver the Christmas bags ourselves on Christmas Day.

Folks all knew we were coming. Little children waited timidly within the homes; eyes wide open, noses pressed flat against the windowpanes. When we approached, some of the smaller ones threw open the door hurriedly and ran eagerly to the Jeep. There was great excitement as the Christmas bag was placed into the tiny and eager hands. Shelby and I spent the entire day delivering the Christmas bags; however, we did take time out to eat a delicious pork chop, biscuit and gravy dinner prepared by Shelby's wife, Mary. Our journey finally ended about six o'clock that evening.

That night, too tired to climb the stairs to my bedroom, I spent the night on the couch in the living room of the manse.

Something had happened that day—something that I would never forget. When we would deliver a Christmas bag at a home, someone—either a child or an adult—came forward and placed a gift in my hands—homemade candy, knitted socks, fruit jars full of jelly, bags of dried shuck beans, homemade handkerchiefs, oatmeal boxes filled with delicious cookies, a mess of meat. All that day I had difficulty in driving, for tears constantly blurred my vision.

He was only seven years of age, but he had memorized perfectly " 'Twas the Night Before Christmas." During practice I held him on my lap while he recited the poem. That night, at the Christmas program before a capacity crowd, he sat on my lap but said nothing. I whispered, "Go ahead, Claude." He muttered, "I don't know it." The problem was intensified because I did not know it, either. Later, I was to learn that his embarrassment was prompted because he had been asked to recite the poem in a pair of pajamas—as though he were going to bed. In overalls, he knew the poem perfectly; but in pajamas, he was silent as a tomb.

Christmas programs were always the hallmark of the Christmas season. Each church beautifully presented the programs, rehearsed to perfection; some with the smaller children; some with the young people. They worked diligently: memorizing, preparing the stage, and decorating the Christmas tree.

I remember well the year the young people at Indian Creek asked if they might be responsible for their own costumes. I was delighted at their initiative, for this took a great responsibility from my shoulders.

Time and time again we rehearsed the Nativity play. They knew their lines perfectly. Not once during rehearsal had we donned costumes, that was being saved for the grand finale—the final presentation!

That night I sat in the back row, deeply proud of the production which I had written personally. Not only was I a Presbyterian minister, I was also a playwright!

When Mary and Joseph walked out on the stage, all of my aspirations as a playwright quickly disappeared. Mary was dressed in a bright red satin dress and loaded with costume jewelry. Never before had I seen such gold (Fort Knox must have been envious!), jewels and rhinestone costume pieces! The Queen of Sheba could not have been so endowed. This was to be Mary's only chance at stardom, and she intended to make the most of it!

He was an old man—tall and thin, an Elder in the Indian Creek Presbyterian Church, and his glasses had the habit of slipping down to the end of his nose. "My wife couldn't come

96

today," he said hesitantly. "So I aim to do the buying." As I held up dresses at our used clothing sale, he would come forward with a piece of baling twine in his hands. "Wait a minute," he would say.

Then, taking the twine, he gently circled it around the dress. "Nope, too large."

Finally he found one to his "liking and dimension" and, after paying fifteen cents for it, he walked back up the road with the dress under his arm and the twine stuck back in his pocket. Someone called out, "Merry Christmas," but he gave no answer as he went joyfully on his way.

In the Jeep, one Christmas day I delivered boxes to several families. There was always someone who was not remembered until the last minute; or someone would call, informing me of a name that had been forgotten. One home left an indelible mark upon me. The father—young, in his early twenties—had been seriously ill in the hospital, but he had returned home to spend the holidays with his wife and small son. Realizing that their Christmas would probably be very bleak, we had prepared a box with apples, oranges, candy and toys. About ten a.m. I drove up to their home. Surprised by my visit (for they had never attended our church), they invited me in. The room was immaculately clean, a fire was burning in the open grate, and under the Christmas tree was one little plastic toy—only *one!* When the child saw the box I had brought, with the large red truck, the little train set and the other toys, no camera on earth could possibly have captured the excitement and the joy beaming from his tiny face. One by one he took each item out of the box, raced over and placed it into the open hands of his father. Then grabbing the mother by the hand, he led her over to the collected toys. Without a doubt, the hour spent in that humble home that Christmas Day was one of the happiest I will ever know here on earth.

Through the years I found great enjoyment in sitting down and personally addressing my Christmas cards to the people of the three churches. Each card had been carefully chosen, for hour after hour would be spent in Lexington at the various stores, trying to find just the right card. *Always* a Hallmark, but *never* too expensive!

One year, after all of the cards had been addressed, one remained. The card had been dropped to the floor and someone had stepped upon it; so, consequently, it kept being pushed to the back of the stack. Finally, looking at the smears on the white envelope, the decision was made to throw it away. Better not to send a card than to send one that was dirty.

Then, suddenly, I remembered an elderly man, whom I did not know too well, who lived up one of the hollows here on the creek. Quickly I addressed the card to him, dirt and all, then mailed it with the rest of the cards and thought no more about the incident.

Several weeks later, while in Booneville, the old man saw me, motioned for me to stop, then quickly walked over to my car. Tenderly he placed his hand on my arm. The face was lined and old and there was gratitude in his eyes.

"Joe, I want to thank you for that Christmas card." He spoke softly, almost in a whisper. "It was the only one I got. I sure do thank you for remembering me."

There is one Christmas Eve program we will never forget. The temperature fell to zero with a wind-chill factor of 40° below zero. Because of the severe cold, the electrical lines broke—about ten minutes prior to our Cow Creek program. Elsie Morris had charge of the program that year, and having just one flashlight, there was much difficulty encountered in getting Mary and Joseph, the Wise Men, the Angels and the Stars all in the proper costumes, but somehow she managed. And, by candlelight, it was without a doubt one of the most beautiful programs ever given in the Cow Creek Church. Christmas morning the temperature fell to 11° below zero—16° below zero over on Indian Creek.

I have always wanted snow for Christmas. To me, it just wasn't really Christmas unless there was snow. One year my wildest expectations and dreams were fulfilled.

As the Candlelight Service and the distribution of Christmas bags were being held, outside the new snow silently accumulated to three or four inches. It seemed strange that no one had thought about checking the weather prior to the service, but as I remember, the night had been clear.

During the service Clyde came to me and said, "Joe, I just looked outside and it is snowing—hard. I think we should all go home before we get snowbound." When I looked out through the window, I quickly agreed to his suggestion.

Everyone had difficulty in getting *off* the hill. And, once off the hill, everyone had as much, or more, trouble in getting *up* the hill on the other side of the creek to the main road. Men and women formed a human chain, and everyone gave a helping hand in "pushing" the cars and trucks. The snow continued to fall—getting deeper by the hour. Having just put on new snow tires, I volunteered to drive as many to their homes as I could; but, this venture proved fruitless when I went off the road just over the hill on the curve beyond Sam Cornett's. Earl and I walked back to Bell's and a wrecker was called. It was just a few minutes before the wrecker appeared and had the car back on the road. Earl's family, unable to get home that night, rode back with me and walked up the hollow. They spent the night with Charlie and Etta Belle here on Cow Creek. No one was able to get up the big hill leading into Booneville; so, that night, everyone stayed with friends or relatives on Cow Creek.

I had prayed for snow, never dreaming that my prayers would be so wonderfully and abundantly answered! However, many persons did not appreciate my happiness and joy.

It became traditional for the young people to go caroling during the week before Christmas. Though it was extremely cold we would bundle up and, with candles in hand and singing a little off-key, we went from home to home, singing for the sick and the elderly. The children loved it, and I, too, felt the joy and spirit of sharing through the ministry of song. As a rule we stayed on hallowed ground, going to those individuals well-known within our area; but, one year we decided the Christian thing to do would be to visit as many elderly persons as possible, so a list was quickly drawn up.

He was an elderly man, and he and his wife lived up one of the hollows on another creek across the mountain. Evidentially they were not aware of the custom of caroling. As we crept silently up to the home, lit the candles, and started singing the beautiful "Silent Night, Holy Night," the old man opened the front door, walked boldly out on the porch with a .38 pistol in his hand and demanded: "What in the hell are you all doing out there?"

Sixteen young people and one Presbyterian minister abruptly ended their singing—halfway through the verse—and made a hasty retreat back to the church van! Hurriedly, the decision was made to return to the manse for hot cocoa; for looking straight into the barrel of a .38 somehow takes the joy out of singing!

In the early years at the Cow Creek Church we would draw names each Christmas, and the custom was that the gift could not be purchased. The donor either had to "make it, bake it, or grow it." I liked the custom, for it was different and unique; but, in time, like everything else, it, too, went its way.

Some of the churches which had a major part in our Christmas sharing were the College Hill Presbyterian Church; the Wyoming Presbyterian Church in Cincinnati; First Presbyterian Church in Perth Amboy, New Jersey; the Coatesville Presbyterian Church, Coatesville, Pennsylvania; the Erin Presbyterian Church, Knoxville, Tennessee; Westminster Presbyterian Church and the Fairmont Presbyterian Church in Dayton, Ohio; Women's Home & Foreign Missionary Society, First Presbyterian Church in Pittsburgh, Pennsylvania; Old First Presbyterian Church, Newark, New Jersey; the Westminster Presbyterian Church, Akron, Ohio; the Lebanon Presbyterian Church, Lebanon, Ohio (which also continued their generous support throughout the year); the Overbrook Presbyterian Church, Columbus, Ohio; the Progress-Immanuel Presbyterian Church of Harrisburg, Pennsylvania; the Church of the Covenant, Washington, Pennsylvania; and the Lewinsville Presbyterian Church of McLean, Virginia.

There was a group in Knoxville, Tennessee, at the Erin Presbyterian Church, that gave much happiness to the people of our area. The Toymakers—founded by Faith Stockdale and originated, I believe, from her Sunday school class —made stuffed toys and animals in autumn and delivered them to Cow Creek just before the Christmas holidays. One item became an instant hit—the stuffed monkey made from a man's sock! This one single item was to give untold happiness, joy and laughter. At first we placed it, as intended in the Christmas bag for the children; but one year, falling short of adult gifts, I placed one of the monkeys in the bag of an Elder. During the Christmas program, when the bag was opened by the Elder, he gave forth with an excited shout:

Bringing home the Christmas tree.

The author and two D.A.R. ladies, following a speaking engagement at the Mayflower Hotel, in Washington, D.C.

"Hey, look what I got!" All eyes in the sanctuary immediately turned toward the cute, loveable, homely little sock monkey which was being held high with admiration and love in the hands of the Elder.

The following year, when the boxes arrived from Erin, after much thought and prayer, the stuffed monkeys were carefully placed aside for a different and very special ministry.

Hereafter, while making hospital calls to the sick and the dying, the sock monkey would give much happiness and joy.

I can well remember walking one evening, just about dusk, up the hollow, carrying a brown paper bag in my hand. The visit was to an elderly woman dying with cancer. A remarkable and beautiful person, a devout Baptist, through the years she had come to our nickel sales at the Indian Creek Church. She was always smiling and I loved her. At one of the sales she had bought a pair of red satin pajamas, which seemed so "out of character" for this devout woman; so there was much kidding and teasing about that particular purchase!

She was waiting on the porch for me, outside, sitting in a rocking chair. It was painful to see her thin face; the thin hands, but the smile was just as beautiful as ever.

"I thought you would never get here," she spoke quietly, almost in a whisper.

"Sorry! At times it is almost impossible for me to keep a schedule," I said, taking her thin hand in mine.

We talked for a long time, and I noticed that her eyes kept moving to the brown paper bag in my hands. Knowing that her curiosity had been aroused, I said nothing.

Finally, she had to ask. "Joe, what do you have in that brown paper bag?"

"It's a little gift I have for you," I answered, placing the bag in her hands.

Slowly, she pulled the stuffed monkey out and immediately her face was brightened with a new radiance. It were as though a light had suddenly been thrust upon her.

Tears filled her eyes and, smiling, she whispered, "I don't know of anything you could have given me that would have given me as much happiness!"

Walking back down the little path to the road, I turned. Sitting on the porch with a shawl around her thin shoulders, she held the monkey in her arms and, then slowly, she raised her hand and waved good-bye.

Several months after my visit she passed away. I was told that, when the end came, she died with the little sock monkey in her arms.

So, the monkeys, made by the women of the Erwin Presbyterian Church in Knoxville, had a special ministry in the hills of Kentucky.

Everett Sebastian lived with Clyde and Lucy in the hollow down from the manse. His wife had left him, and his two children lived with their grandparents in another country. A quiet man, who had asthma, he did odd jobs helping Clyde on the farm.

Always at Christmas, Everett gave me a present, usually a pair of socks, either too large or too small, or a handkerchief, wrapped in a brown paper bag; but his small gift meant as much to me as any gift I received.

The Christmas bags were delivered on Christmas Day to our shut-ins, and the recipients received just as much happiness and joy as did the children. Her name was Belle Cornett, ninety-four years of age, and she had taught the young people's Sunday school class for years and years. When the new road was being built here on Cow Creek, and I was

Cow Creek children with Christmas bags.

unable to take my car down for her on Sunday morning, she had walked through the mud in order to attend church and to teach her class.

Knowledgeable, likeable, deeply religious (her brother, Preacher Ike, was one of the most beloved and respected ministers in our area), eagerly she accepted the colored Christmas bag, untied the string, and brought forth the articles within—a shawl, toilet articles, handkerchiefs, fruit, candy and stationery.

She smiled, "Thank you, Joe. Thank you!"

There was a pause, a hesitation for a few minutes. Almost inaudibly she continued, "I was really hoping that I might get a doll!"

A doll for a ninety-four-year-old woman? All of the dolls had been given away. Not a single one remained, for they had all gone to the little girls of the three churches!

After prayer, I went back to the church. Could there be one more doll? Would it be possible to find just one? The door to the Christmas Room was opened—the one room behind the sanctuary—but Santa's Workshop was bare. Nothing remained but scattered papers, boxes, and a few coloring books.

There might possibly be an unopened box at the manse. At the end of the couch were several boxes filled with mittens which we had planned to share with the children of the local elementary school. The boxes had all been opened and had contained mittens, but there was one box *still wrapped,* and it was *insured!*

Excitedly, I tore into the brown box. Inside, carefully and lovingly wrapped in white tissue paper was one of the most beautiful dolls I had ever seen! The box contained only the doll. Immediately I searched the outside of the box for the name of the donor, but the name had previously been cut off and placed into a large box with the rest of the names. I wanted to write a special letter thanking that individual or church for such a wonderful gift!

Within twenty minutes I was back down at Belle's and, when she saw the doll, she cried out with joy! Sitting by the open fireplace, this ninety-four-year-old woman, holding her doll, was a picture I wish I could have captured with my camera; but, somehow, it just did not seem the right thing to do at the time. So, I simply wished her a Merry Christmas and went on my way!

One year the following article appeared in *Concern,* the official magazine of the United Presbyterian Women:

OPERATION CRADLE

For some people Christmas came early this year! As a matter of fact, for the Gay 90s—a group of retirement-age folks at Central Presbyterian Church in McKeesport, Pennsylvania—preparations for this year's Christmas started early in January. Now, if you promise not to let this magazine fall into the hands of the children of the Cow Creek churches in Kentucky, we'll tell you this amazing story of love in action. We just wouldn't want those youngsters to find out that some of Santa's helpers are not little gnomes working at the North Pole, but, rather are real live grandmas and grandpas who live in McKeesport, Pennsylvania.

Actually, this story begins several years ago—and it grew out of the fact that Millie Stang, the preacher's wife at Central, can't sew very well. Central's Women's Association has an amazing program of "second mile" handiwork, wherein the women literally turn out thousands of items for sending to mission stations. While Mrs. Stang had organized, encouraged, and promoted this program from its beginning, she had never contributed too much of her own handiwork. One day several years ago she was struck with the idea of putting her woodworking hobby to use. She decided to make a wooden doll cradle and subsequently turned it in for exhibit at the Association meeting, along with the usual handiwork projects. There were some comments and expressions of interest, but the original effort went by pretty much unnoticed. A few more cradles were made and sent out at Christmas, but without much comment either at home or from the recipients.

In the meantime, the Gay 90s had been organized by this same woodworking preacher's wife. The men of this small group were encouraged to try their hands at the cradle project. The women readily took up the task of providing the bedding needed—handmade mattresses, sheets, pillows, and tiny patchwork quilts.

Here the story begins to take a more personal and intense turn. At the 171st General Assembly in Indianapolis last year, the Stangs met one of the National Missions pastors to whom Central women had been sending "second mile" handiwork for several years. They were immediately attracted to the Reverend Joe Powlas, who is pastor at Cow Creek and Indian Creek in the hills of Kentucky. Subsequently, an invitation was issued for Mr. Powlas to visit McKeesport in October of the same year as a speaker at the Women's Association meeting. Mr. Powlas readily accepted. Before returning home from his visit in McKeesport, he was introduced to the Association handiwork chairman and, since he would soon have been mailed a box of handiwork for his Christmas program, it was decided that it would save postage and packing to send the gifts to Cow Creek with the pastor on his trip home. He needed utility bags—and there were fifty or so on hand. He could use stuffed toys—and there were two big boxes full to choose from. And, by this time, there were five or six cradles. Could he use them? Could he! So, off he went, loaded with gifts, leaving behind a church that had taken him and his work completely to their hearts.

Less than a week later, the women at Central got an S.O.S. letter from Joe Powlas. "You said, 'Just ask.' " he wrote, "so I'm asking! Could I please have twenty-five more cradles? I just couldn't decide who, among all my little girls, shouldn't get a cradle. Could you possibly make one for *each* of my little girls?"

Twenty-five! Mrs. Stang was flabbergasted. Certainly, she herself could hardly make three or four more before Christmas. It was already the first week in November. Harry Winklevoss, the craft chairman for the men of the Gay 90s, caught the spirit and said his group would try—but could they *possibly* make so many before Christmas? What about enlisting the help of some of the other men of the church?

The following Sunday morning, armed with sets of roughly drawn plans, Mrs. Stang approached the Men's Bible Class—would they help? Half a dozen or so took plans that day. By Wednesday morning, cradles began arriving at the manse and the church; some finished, others needing only painting and decorating. By the following Sunday, there was a dozen or more to display. Other men, some of whom are not able to get to church any more, heard of the project and sent for directions through their sons. Some needed wood provided. In two weeks, with much telephoning and organizing of painting parties—and with the women of the Gay 90s busy sewing—the cradle table in Fellowship Hall was piled high. The local newspaper sent a photographer and the resultant publicity had the whole town talking.

Now, how to ship them? Huge cartons were obtained, piles of newspapers were brought in, and the Gay 90s—some of whom are in their 80s—gathered at the church for an all-

110

day packing session. Finally, the cradles were ready to go. along with the many dolls which had somehow turned up to fill the cradles, and with many a prayer that they would arrive in time for Christmas, the shipment left for Cow Creek, Kentucky.

This story has a happy ending. The cradles did arrive in time and, if the smiles on the faces of the little girls as they were photographed by this missionary pastor are any indication, it was truly a Merry Christmas for all of them.

In McKeesport, it was even happier, for the people in Central Church had learned a new dimension in stewardship. Mr. Winklevoss said, "We got more fun out of doing it than those children could possibly get out of our simple cradles." As "Wink" spoke, he was remembering, no doubt, many a happy evening spent in his workshop fashioning the cradles he himself produced while his wife Leolia sewed away at tiny quilts and blankets.

The real happiness of this story is that it has no ending. By the time the Gay 90s came together for their regular meeting, the second week in January this year, they were already making plans for Christmas of next year. What those plans are, we can't say, for that's a secret. But, of this you can be sure: Santa still has an outpost workshop in McKeesport, and it's not likely to close up for a long time. Christmas not only comes early at Central Church; it seems as though the Christmas spirit has become a year-round affair.

That year, we had a special wonderful Christmas!

I cannot remember his name, nor do I remember the church nor the state; but, retired, he made over one hundred wooden trucks for our Christmas bags, and then he and his wife brought them by pickup truck to Cow Creek. Beautifully and perfectly constructed, they gave much happiness and joy to our little boys. Hopefully, he will get some extra stars in his crown!

While hurrying to a ministerial meeting in Booneville one year, I decided to drop off several Christmas bags to some children who, although they lived in Clay County, had visited Cow Creek from time to time. So, the bags were placed in my car and I quickly drove up the hollow.

The children were outside in the yard playing, but when I emerged from the car with the Christmas bags, they came running, laughing and calling, "Joe, Joe, Joe! You remembered us!"

Each child was given a bag. Their smiles were unbelievable! The children, ages four, six, and eight, had never been so happy.

In unison, they carefully placed the Christmas bags on the ground, ran to where I was standing, then they hugged me as I had never been hugged before. They hugged my legs; they hugged me as I picked each of them up; they hugged my arms; and even hugged the top of my head! But, alas! Each child had been eating a peanut butter and jelly sandwich and I was smeared from head to foot.

There was no time for changing clothes; so, quickly, I went my way—the "sweetest minister in Owsley County."

The Christmas bags were something special, giving great joy to the young and old alike. As a church leader, I was so grateful for this ministry; grateful that we could share so beautifully the love of Christ; grateful to those churches, and to those individuals who so generously shared with our yearly project of five hundred and fifty Christmas bags!

Each year I fell on my knees and gave thanks to the Lord for this part of our ministry!

7

During the years of my ministry four dogs and a horse were to have special places within my heart.

One day Joe Fed Baker, who lived up the creek, was at the manse. This tiny lad was deeply admired because he was the only person I ever knew who could run and mount a horse or pony from the rear. He would take one jump, place his hands on the rump of the horse, landing squarely on its back. That, to me, was spectacular!

Joe Fed calmly announced that day that every preacher needed a dog. Without further explanation he turned and walked over the hill. Sometime later this small boy from Crane Fork returned with the most adorable pup I had ever seen. It was love at first sight, and we named him Shadrack.

Shadrack, in time, became the largest dog in Owsley County and should have earned a record in the *Guinness Book of Records.* A mongrel, his one desire in life was to eat, and there was nothing that he would not consume! The children loved Shadrack, spending hours riding on his back, pulling his tail, playing fetch the ball, and hide and seek. Playful, loveable, and friendly, he was to create a unique niche in the life of Cow Creek.

Belle Cornett had given me a chicken, already cut up, ready for the frying pan. I cherished that chicken, eating two pieces at a time. I was down to the last two pieces and while eating my lunch one day, a fellow minister from Booneville came up on the hill. Now the hospitable thing to have done would have been to invite him in and share my chicken with him; but, quickly, I raced to the door and met him on the porch, and we chatted there for about fifteen minutes.

After the visit had been concluded, I rushed back to the kitchen to finish my meal; but, alas! The plate was clean. Nothing remained, either on the plate or on the table. Storming out the kitchen door I found Shadrack sleeping on the steps as though nothing had happened.

The first divorce of my ministry came about because of Shadrack. For a number of years my record had been without blemish, and there was much pride in the fact that all of my marriages had endured—that none had ended in divorce. But that record was not to last.

Church weddings in Cow Creek were to be rare, so I well remember this one. The groom, a special friend of mine on the creek, was nervous but I assured him that nothing could go wrong. There was nothing to worry about, because the service would only last a few minutes and soon he and his bride would be on their way to eternal bliss!

Everything went well until I came to the phrase: "Do you take this man to be your lawful wedded husband?" Shadrack raced down the aisle—the doors had been left open—jumped up, placed his paws on my shoulders and, in so doing, knocked the bride to the floor.

Hurriedly we helped the young girl to her feet and put Shadrack out of the church; but the bride was angry, hurt that a dog had ruined her wedding. Their marriage lasted only a short time. It is my firm belief that the bride never thought, nor felt, that she had really and truly been married.

Shadrack, in time, became an integral part of our Five and One-Half Club. He was always there to greet the

The beloved Monkey Sock doll.

children when they came for their weekly meeting at the manse.

Usually, there were games and the memorizing of the *Shorter Catechism,* but one night Marjorie Rawling's *The Yearling* was playing at the local drive-in theater on the other side of Booneville and since it was Family Night, a carload could be taken in for two dollars.

So sixteen kids and a preacher got into my old black car. One little boy looked out of the car window at Shadrack, who sat sadly nearby. "Shadrack ain't never been to a movie. Let's take Shadrack."

It took a lot of maneuvering and pushing but finally, the huge dog, with great glee, settled down within the car—along with sixteen kids and one preacher.

Then the door was closed on Shadrack's tail. Pandemonium broke loose for a few seconds until the door could be opened. Luckily none of the children were bitten, but Shadrack would never again enter a car.

Once a year the Ows-Lee Parish Presbyterian Women met at Cow Creek. It was a quarterly meeting and women came from Booneville, Indian Creek, Beattyville, St. Helen's and Mount Paran, from Lee County. A potluck lunch was customary, and since the church had no kitchen, the women would leave their food down at the manse until it was time to eat in the back room of the church.

Who could ever forget Mollie Baker's green cake that day? It was a very odd shade of green, the exact color had never been seen before!

Up on the hill, as I sat in the back pew during the service, I had a terrible feeling that something was wrong; so, quietly, while Lily Kincaid was speaking, I left the sanctuary.

The front door of the manse was open—we had no screen doors—and in the kitchen, Shadrack was up on the table, in

116

all his glory, his left hind leg in a pumpkin pie, eating Mollie Baker's green cake.

Getting Shadrack off the table was not an easy task. Finally, outside, I gave him the rest of the cake. Then, quickly, taking the palm of my hand I smoothed out the pumpkin pie as best I could, placing it on the edge of the table, far-removed from the more noticeable desserts.

Mollie Baker never mentioned the disappearance of her green cake, and every bit of the pumpkin pie was eaten with great relish!

But I was angry at Shadrack and my anger continued. I was tired of his constant hunger, tired of his escapades, and tired of the problems he was creating; so, a few days later, Shadrack was given to a family who lived on the other side of Booneville.

One can never forget the hurt, the sadness in his eyes as he left the manse that day. He was tied up in the back of a truck and, time and time again, he tried to free himself—jerking at the rope. He looked at me beggingly. Even as the truck drove over the hill I could hear his whimpering, and that sound remained within my mind for a long, long time.

Word came several months later that Shadrack was dead. It is my belief that he died of a broken heart.

The children never forgave me for giving Shadrack away, and I was to live with that guilt—and the sad look in his eyes as he had gone over the hill—for many years.

But in time another dog was to come to Cow Creek and, she, too, would steal the hearts of the children.

I was in Washington, Pennsylvania, visiting in the home of Peg and Lew Hays. They had become interested in dogs—boxers—and when the offer came that I might have one of the pups from the litter, there was great joy. The most beautiful puppy that was available was carefully chosen.

Trips were made to the veterinarian; her ears were clipped, and she became known as Becky.

One day an elderly man here on the creek approached me with great excitement. "Joe, I just saw the most horrible looking dog I've ever seen. Someone cut off his ears, mashed in his face, and he didn't have a tail." True, Becky was quite different from the hounds of the area.

My second boxer was known as Johnny Brown. Johnny Brown had class—ribbons, papers, trophies, and, in every sense of the word, dignity and beauty.

Sarah Lesnett, from Bridgeville, Pennsylvania, was a frequent visitor to Cow Creek. One year as she and her sister, Grace, were departing back to Bridgeville, Sarah turned and asked, "Joe, what do you want personally? I am not talking about the needs of the church, I'm talking about *you*. What do *you* want personally?"

Becky had died with cancer, and I had really been impressed by the boxer; so, my reply had been: "Sarah, I would love to have another boxer dog."

"Good. I will see what can be done."

Several months later the telephone rang and Sarah was on the line, excited.

"Joe, a couple I know is moving from their huge home into an apartment in Pittsburgh, and they have a beautiful boxer, but they cannot take him with them. He's yours—if you can come and get him immediately."

Frank Leasure had once promised several of the boys on the creek that, if they should ever be in Pittsburgh, he would take them to see the Pittsburgh Pirates play. Of course, there was no possibility that they could ever get to Pittsburgh—until they learned that I was going to Bridgeville to get a dog. Pittsburgh was not far from Bridgeville.

They pleaded with me, "Can we go with you?"

"I would love to take you. But you will have to ask *both* your father and mother. If they *both* say 'yes,' then it will be all right with me." The parents agreed that the boys could go.

A telephone call was made to Frank and Marie Leasure, informing them that I was coming to Bridgeville. Could they, and would they, keep three boys for the night? And would Frank take them to see the Pittsburgh Pirates play? (I prayed that there would be a game that night. There was!)

So, happily and hurriedly, Willis McIntosh, Roger Roberts, Johnny Combs and I got in the car and headed for Pennsylvania.

Every so often we would stop for a break. Once, we got some sandwiches and pop and had a picnic by the river. Following the meal, I was putting the left-overs back in the car when I discovered Willis, about fourteen or fifteen years of age, swimming out in the middle of the river. It was a wide river and he was several hundred feet from shore. Never had I been so frightened, and never before in all my life had I prayed so hard. An excellent swimmer, I knew that he could easily have replaced Johnny Weismuller as Tarzan, but my fear was that he might unexpectedly develop a cramp. Frantically, I jumped up and down and waved and screamed until he came back to shore, but during those moments I aged ten years.

Once in Bridgeville, a call was made to Frank, who quickly came for the boys. As they headed toward Pittsburgh to watch the Pittsburgh Pirates, there was great happiness and much laughter.

After the boys had gone, Sarah took me around behind the house to see the boxer.

The dog was perfect in every respect—satin coat, meticulously groomed, and nails trimmed. One knew immediately that he had come from a wealthy family, who had taken great pride in his appearance.

For a moment I simply stood and admired him, unable to believe that I actually owned such a dog. Never in my wildest dreams had I expected such a beautiful animal.

With great joy I reached out with my hand to pat him on the head; but with a fierce growl, he snapped at me, missing my fingers by inches. I jumped back in fear! That dog was vicious! Time and time again I tried to approach him, but each time he growled and tried to bite me.

The dog was too beautiful to leave behind, but how could I get him back to Kentucky without being bitten?

That night, before going to bed, Sarah said confidently, "Joe, I know what we will do. You go on up to bed."

Heartbroken and disappointed, I climbed the stairs and tucked myself into the huge four-postered bed.

Then Sarah opened the door. The dog was on a leash. She brought him into the bedroom and left him sitting in the middle of the room. Before leaving, she said, "If you two sleep in the same room together, *maybe* you will become friends."

What happened if we did not become friends? Actually, I was too frightened to give myself an answer. That dog would tear me apart. Was she crazy? If I were going to die, I wanted to die in Kentucky.

Quickly, I pulled the covers over my head and lay there terrified. What if I had to get up to go to the bathroom? No one else slept upstairs. Would anyone hear my cries for help? Two bites from that dog and a man would bleed to death! About an hour later, something jumped up onto the foot of the bed. My first impulse was that it had been an elephant. I realized, of course, that it was the dog. Lying at the foot of the bed, he was king of the roost, and I dared not move an inch! What a dilemma!

I never slept a wink that night. Every so often I would

turn over—moving slowly, by degrees. I had never in my life been so grateful to see the light of morning.

Sarah pecked on the door before coming in. "Good morning, Joe. How did you sleep?"

"I didn't," was my weak reply.

"Take the leash and see what happens."

Strange, but in that moment I had no fear. Boldly, I reached down and took the leash, patted the boxer on the head, and said, "Okay, boy, let's go. You're going back to Kentucky."

Triumphantly, I brought the dog downstairs and took him out in the yard.

When the boys returned we started back to Kentucky. With love and pride we put the boxer in the back seat; but, when the boys started to get in beside him, he growled and snapped at them. So, four of us rode in the front seat all the way back home. No one ventured to sit in the back seat.

In time, Johnny Brown settled down to the quietness and the beauty of Kentucky. No longer was his coat groomed. No longer were his nails polished and clipped, but he grew to love Cow Creek and continuously played with children and adults alike.

Only once did he ever present a problem. Peter McIntosh came down one day to get a bag of apples from the large tree in the yard of the manse. Peter filled the bag and had it in his arms. He had started back toward the road when Johnny Brown jumped up and ran at him. Luckily, I was able to get Johnny Brown off Peter before any damage was done. I presume the dog thought the man was stealing the apples and he was simply being protective.

Always whenever I returned from going into Lexington or Booneville, Johnny Brown would be waiting for me in the window, his hind legs on the couch, the large square face looking toward the road. Never once did I come on the hill but that he was there, waiting.

In time, my love for the dog grew greatly. It was great fun going into Booneville with Johnny Brown sitting in the front seat of the car. People would stare. He always sat with such dignity, and he loved to ride. One day I put an old hat on him, got some black-rimmed glasses, removed the glass, then taped them to his head. Slowly I drove through Booneville, around the square, with the huge boxer sitting in the front seat with great dignity, wearing black-rimmed glasses and an old hat. That was one day that cannot be forgotten.

The people laughed, thinking that it was a great joke; but I am sure there were those who looked and saw a distinguished visitor—a stately gentleman from out of state!

Johnny Brown became ill after five years. Although he was taken to the veterinarian time and time again, one could see that he no longer had the strength he had once possessed and, often, he collapsed on the ground. One day I returned from Booneville and he was not in the window, waiting as he always was.

Frantically a search was made—inside and outside the manse, and I finally found him in the backyard, dead. Although a grown man, I cried with a broken heart, for it was as though a member of my family had passed away. Jimmy Herald came up on the hill and found me beside the manse with Johnny Brown in my arms.

"I can't bury him, Jimmy, I just can't," I sobbed. "Would you please take him up the hollow for me?"

"Yes, Joe, I will," He replied. He got a wheelbarrow and tenderly we lifted the dog up and placed him in the bed.

As he started pushing the wheelbarrow around the manse, I ran and caught him. "No, Jimmy. Wait! I'll do it. I know that *he* would want *me* to bury him. Thanks, but I just can't let anyone else do it. I have to do it myself."

So, with a shovel lying beside him, I pushed Johnny Brown up the hollow. I asked Jimmy not to accompany me, telling him that I wanted to go alone.

I dug the hole, then gently placed my beloved Johnny Brown in and filled the grave. And I cried, every step of the way.

When the youth groups first came to Cow Creek, we always went over to Indian Creek to ride Sam Thomas's mules. This, truly, was the highlight of the week. Our local boys delighted in holding the timid girls safe and secure on the mules, riding behind them.

While speaking to the Mary E. Sage Circle at the Second Presbyterian Church in Lexington one year, the group asked, "Joe, what do you need?"

"A mule," was my quick reply. The ladies were startled, thinking that my needs would be for clothing, Christmas gifts, or some special project.

"A mule?" They asked, with disbelief.

"A mule," I replied calmly.

Two hundred dollars was given to me for the purchase of a mule, after I had explained why I wanted that specific item. Actually, the money bought a horse—not a mule—and I immediately named *him* Mary, after the founder of the circle. Technically, *he* was a horse; consequently, the feminine name seemed most inappropriate; but the ladies, when they learned what I had done, felt that naming a horse after the founder of their circle was disrespectful. So, *Mary* became known as *Toby*.

Toby was a wonderful, unexplainable horse. A shed was built for him near the Summer White House, and an electric fence was put around the ball field where Toby lived in all of his glory. The kids loved him. Since I did not have a saddle, he was always ridden bareback. He, in turn, loved the kids

123

and they would ride him morning, noon, and night. When kids from the visiting youth groups left, they took with them many happy memories of Toby, and probably, a few horse hairs!

One winter, we prepared our Christmas bags in the Summer White House. Tables were made out of plywood, the boxes were sorted, and the bags were prepared on the girls' side. (This place of preparation proved to be disastrous since it became almost impossible to get the gifts out through the mud for our Christmas programs. We tried using a tractor for hauling, but that, too, became stuck.)

One day we were all busy working with our Christmas sorting when Toby walked through the open door. I had never seen a horse inside of a house before. Immediately, he began poking his nose in all of the boxes. We tried to push him, we tried to pull him—but to no avail. He was having the time of his life, and he certainly had no intention of going back outside when all the dolls, balls, and toys were there in front of him.

For over an hour we tried to get Toby to go back outside, but he absolutely refused. How does one get a horse out of a building? Quite simply. Place a piece of peppermint candy in front of his nose and he will follow obediently.

Toby was with us for many, many years.

My last dog was Joby, a St. Bernard. I discovered that, while boxers are brilliant and intelligent, St. Bernards are dumb and loveable—at least Joby was. He grew to immense proportions and was one of the largest dogs I have ever seen. Affectionate, kind and gentle, we all loved him dearly!

One day, Arvis and I discovered several piles of dirt around the Cow Creek Church. At first we thought they were mole holes; then, after digging in them, we discovered that our new church hymnals had been taken from the sanctuary, one by one, and Joby had buried them. Evidently, he did not like our singing!

Joby had a habit of slowly wiggling between a person's legs. This was cute when he was a small dog, but as he became larger it became quite a problem, and I always had the fear that some sweet, little old lady would suddenly be taken for a ride down the hill on the back of a huge St. Bernard!

Joby suddenly disappeared one day and, though we searched the entire creek, he was never again seen. In all probability he was stolen.

8

On April 12, 1945, President Franklin Delano Roosevelt died from a cerebral hemorrhage while at Warm Springs, Georgia. The cortege, making its way by train back to Washington, stopped for thirty minutes at the Southern Railroad Station in Salisbury, North Carolina. As a student at Catawba College, I joined thousands of other mourners who stood silently and respectfully on the platform where, inside, one could see the flag-draped casket of the President of the United States. An honor guard of soldiers from Fort Bragg stood at attention in front of the train.

Years later I learned that, on that night, I had stood within fifty feet of Hays Gabbard, a soldier from Kentucky, who was later to become an Elder in the Indian Creek Presbyterian Church.

When my ministry began at Indian Creek, the old building had broken windows and a door that would not close. The potbellied stove gave out heat, but it was impossible to adequately warm a buidling into which cold air flowed so freely.

What we lacked in material blessings, we possessed spiritually, for ours was a happy church and we were a happy group.

I remember those days so well. For a few minutes I sit alone and my mind wanders back to the little white church where, on Sunday afternoons, we worshipped the Lord. The piano was badly out of tune, but, joyfully, a young minister would belt out the old gospel hymns. There was a wonderful group of young people who met every Thursday night, playing Flying Dutchman, Snatch the Bacon, and a host of other games, but Flying Dutchman was the favorite. A large circle was formed; two persons circled the group, tagged the joined hands of two individuals, then ran in opposite directions. Grabbing a partner from one of those tagged, the couple who got back to the original position first was the winner. Hour after hour we played, and the young people looked forward to C.E. just as much as I.

Early one Thursday, Lucy Eversole called and wanted to know if her minister could possibly take her to Lexington to the doctor. Yes, I could; however, we had to be back that night for C.E. at Indian Creek. On the way there was the sudden realization that her minister had no spare tire, and all four tires on the car were extremely thin. Humbly, a prayer was offered that my tires would not go flat—that I would get Lucy to her appointment.

Then on the way back the silent prayers continued, the petition being that we might get back to Cow Creek without incident. No one will believe this story (fact truly is stranger than fiction!), but after getting Lucy back home, then driving over to the Indian Creek Church where the young people were waiting for me, when I stepped from the car *a front tire went flat!*

Such were the early days!

Junior, Dale and Billy Wilder; Norm and Alma Roberts; Nazalee, Marvin and Andy Bowling; Emma Jean and Ruth Cole; Buck and Marcus Thomas; Pauline, June, Addie, and Tommy Thomas; Kaye Steppe; Lela Eversole; Gail and

Carol Burton; Nedra, Monte, Jerome, Fayette, and Albert—
I see them all now so vividly, as we walked up-and-down the
road, arm in arm, singing, laughing and talking. We had no
money, but we possessed a richness that gave us joy, happiness and fun!

During my early years I had much difficulty in keeping
my car running. One Ford I possessed really caused me a lot
of embarrassment, for it smoked continuously, even though
oil had to be put in twice as often as gasoline! When I was going through Booneville, my head would be ducked as low as
possible, all the while praying that perhaps the people would
not see that the car was being driven by the new minister
from North Carolina; however, the smoking vehicle always
drew their attention and, probably, a few laughs.

The car quit quite often—anywhere, anytime, any place,
but it had a special preference for quitting on Indian Creek.
A telephone call would be made to Cliff Riley, who lived on
Cow Creek. In an hour or two Cliff would drive up and, with
a piece of baling wire, a hammer, and a pair of pliers, the car,
through his hammering and twisting, would be in running
order again.

"How much do I owe you?" I would ask.

"About fifty cents—or a dollar," would be his reply. He
always came, and he would get paid—but back then, a dollar
was an astronomical fee!

The women quilted weekly on Indian Creek, making
beautiful works of art. Each Monday they were picked up in
my car then, several hours later, taken home.

One day, while taking the women home, the car quit. I
asked the ladies if any of them could drive. None of them
could. So, I had no choice. I would do the driving but, out of
necessity, they would have to get out and get behind the car
and push, in order to enable me to "kick it off." Had anyone

passed us at that particular time, that person would certainly have been amused as well as perplexed—a grown man sitting in a car while seven women were behind it, pushing.

An elderly man on Indian Creek bought a new truck, but he had never learned to drive. "Joe," Lewis Cole asked me one day, "would you help me learn to drive?"

Lewis and Lily were wonderful people. Good, kind, and deeply devout, they attended our church regularly although they were Baptist.

"Sure, Lewis, I will be glad to."

So, we went down to the bottom, tobacco sticks were put up, a road was staked out, and, hour after hour, day after day, Lewis, behind the wheel, tried out his new truck. At first, he was hesitant, but gradually, as he drove, he gained more confidence, and when he went for his driving test, he passed without any problems.

One cold January day, when the temperature was 10° above zero, Andy Bowling, Thelma Gabbard, Wilson Thomas and I were sitting around the potbellied stove after church. It was then and there that a decision was made to build a new church. The old church would be torn down and a new church would be built. Since our Sunday offerings were never more than three or four dollars this dream seemed almost an impossibility, but we had faith and determination. After consulting with the minister in Booneville who, at that time, was the head of the Ows-Lee Presbyterian Parish, we decided to tear the old building down when spring came.

During the interim period—before a new structure was put up—we met, as weather permitted, in the cemetery. There under the heavens, beneath the large oak tree, Sunday after Sunday we worshipped sitting on logs.

I remember being in Pennsylvania and, after the service,

the minister was showing me the church. It was a beautiful building. Proudly, he took me in a room and remarked, "This room alone cost more than twenty thousand dollars!" Twenty thousand dollars! There were crystal chandeliers from France, a beautiful Steinway grand piano, and a silver tea service—while, on Sunday, our people were sitting on logs to worship.

It took more than twenty-six years to complete our little Indian Creek Church. Local people came in and worked, and the women brought in dinner. We moved slowly—little by little.

Once the roof had been put up, homemade benches were made by the Elders of our church, and I commended them for the good job. Still, the benches needed painting. Paint was bought from a local store (I was unaware that cheap paint could be disastrous!), and the benches were painted a dark black. From the pulpit they looked beautiful, giving a dignified look to the sanctuary.

The following Sunday the temperature inside the church was extremely hot, the women perspired freely and the cheap paint came off the benches onto the women's best dresses; and for once, every woman in the Indian Creek Church was angry at Joe Powlas.

Frank Leasure, an electrician from Bridgeville, Pennsylvania, wired the new building. Tile for the sanctuary came from the Youth Fellowship of the Fairmont Presbyterian Church of Dayton, Ohio, who came to Cow Creek and spent a week with us. From the Lewinsville Presbyterian Church, in McLean, Virginia, we received a beautiful new Baldwin spinet piano. In time, a beautiful red carpet was received, through the love and concern of the Shenango Presbyterial, of Pennsylvania.

We had no hymnals—I mimeographed song sheets—so

131

an appeal went out to supporting churches: "Do you have any hymn books you no longer need?" Within a few weeks, word came that 200 hymnals would be sent to us. Hallelujah! We rejoiced at our good fortune. When they came, however, shipped by freight to Beattyville, they arrived C.O.D. It took several offerings to raise enough money to get the books from the depot. (I later learned that the donor church had an annual budget of over one hundred thousand dollars.) Anyway, we had our hymnals; so, the following Sunday, we opened the books and sang. They were Presbyterian hymnals and, although *I* knew most of the hymns—having grown up in a large beautiful church at Crossnore, North Carolina—our Indian Creek congregation knew only *five* hymns contained within the books. Sunday after Sunday, we sang the same five hymns.

One day a lady sent a check for fifty dollars and, immediately, fifty gospel hymn books were ordered, which included such old favorites as "The Old Rugged Cross," "In the Garden," "When the Roll Is Called Up Yonder," etc.

We conducted our Vacation Bible Schools outside. Under the large oak at the entrance of the cemetery, I taught the Young People's Class. In the beginning we had no teaching materials, so I simply used the Bible. The young people sat on the ground, listening attentively. Grace Shaw and her sister, Sarah, came down from Bridgeville, Pennsylvania, and the three of us taught the Vacation Bible Schools. We soon encountered a difficulty. In the Primary Class, the mothers were so eager, enthused and delighted with what the small ones were doing, they ended up doing the work themselves, and the smaller children simply sat and watched.

Tactfully, with Margaret Ronaldson, we started the Mother's Class, not only teaching them the Bible, but also sharing crafts with them; and, in time, the Mother's Class became one of our most popular classes.

Anyone could attend Bible School, and just about everyone did. One man—Bill Bowling, eighty-one years of age—came to Vacation Bible School regularly and we were delighted and honored by his presence. We often had one hundred and fifty or more enrolled for these earlier years. All of this was remarkable when one considers that, at that time, we had no water and no toilet facilities at the church!

The big event of the day was the ball game. Everyone loved softball, and the games were played in the cemetery with home plate being just below the oak tree. We did not consider it irreverent nor sacrilegious that the outfield reached deep among the graves.

One day while playing in a softball game, one of the boys became extremely furious. When questioned, he remarked, "I would have made a home run had it not been for Uncle Henry."

I well understood his perplexity. The ball had hit Uncle Henry's tombstone, bounced back, and the outfielder had quickly thrown the ball to home plate.

The little church was extremely generous. At Christmas, underneath the brightly lit tree on the stage there would always be numerous packages, beautifully wrapped, containing homemade cookies, candy, shaving kits, shirts, and books and socks. Each year the church always gave me one present—something special! Usually Nazalee would ask, "What would you like for Christmas this year?"

The answer would be, "Anything, just anything."

Sometimes I would suggest a gift I especially wanted: a tripod for my camera, or several rolls of 35mm film, etc. It is

Summer White House and Toby.

really hard to keep a secret from a minister, because everyone wants to tell you what no one else is supposed to know, consequently, I always knew what would be forthcoming.

One year, Nazalee failed to ask the routine question. I thought that, since there were so many individual presents, there really was no need for a special present from the church, and financially, we needed every dollar to meet our obligations; so, I thought no more about it.

That year at our Christmas Program there was a large package on the stage. Tucked beneath the bright ribbon was the name "Joe Powlas." This was one secret that I was never told about beforehand. No one had told me a thing. To be perfectly honest I was happy, or happier, than any little child that evening. At the end of the program Laura Thomas came forward and made a little announcement: The church had a special present for the minister. She presented it to me and instructed that it be opened.

The string was untied, the paper removed, and there in my hands was the most beautiful quilt I had ever seen. The pattern was the Little Dutch Girl, and each square had been autographed in colored thread. Tearfully I read: Lula Thomas, Cora Yeary, Emma Jean Wilson, Flora Callahan, June Marshall, Norma Lee Thomas, Viola Marshall, Leta M. Giancola, Nannie Peters, Belle Mayes, Lela Bishop, Rosa Bowling, Lela Keller, Rosa Gabbard, Laura Thomas, Ida Callahan, Agnes Gabbard, Thelma Gabbard, Bertie Gabbard, Nancy Callahan, Dolly Marshall, June Gabbard, Regina Robinson, Helen Gabbard, Lily Cole, Nannie Thomas, Pauline Gabbard, Grace Bowling, Verna Gabbard, and Nazalee Tirey.

That was a Christmas I will long remember—and treasure.

She was an older woman, and she and her husband faithfully attended church every Sunday. Although her husband had a moderate income, I was told that he placed only two pennies in the collection plate every Sunday, his reasoning being that the widow gave only two mites to the Lord. (What was good enough for the widow was good enough for him!)

She seemed so sad, so distant, yet so kind and gentle. One Sunday, as I stood at the door shaking hands, I casually remarked, "What a beautiful dress you have on today!"

Immediately, her face shone, she smiled, and she was so pleased by my compliment. It was as though someone had given her a beautiful gift!

The following Sunday, although her husband came to church, she was absent. Thinking that, perhaps she might have company, I said nothing. The second Sunday, again I noticed that she was absent, but she had children in Ohio and Indiana, so I presumed that she was visiting with them.

The third Sunday, again she was absent; so, as the husband left, I asked about his wife. He remarked that she had been under the weather but was feeling much better. Several persons who heard our conversation waited until the man left, then drew me aside.

"He won't let her come to church because you bragged on her dress. He thinks you are flirting with her." I sat down in disbelief.

She returned to our services exactly one month later. As she and her husband came out of the church, I shook her hand—but I kept my mouth *shut!*

He was a large man with a beard, and he wore a black hat. When the Black Brothers bus had pulled into Booneville my first day in Owsley County, he was the first person I had seen, standing silently, leaning against the courthouse wall, knife in hand, whittling on a piece of wood, and chewing tobacco. As I walked nervously past him with my cardboard suitcase in hand, his look was as cold as steel, and I felt, at twenty-three years of age, like a small child, so frail and so fragile, too weak to begin a ministry in Kentucky!

In time, we became friends and he seemed to like me, though I often thought that, perhaps, he was toying with me as a cat toys with a mouse—just seeking to devour its prey. He had a large, devoted following who, Sunday after Sunday, walked behind their leader obediently and faithfully. Their place of meeting was up the hollow past our church. Many a Sunday, as they passed by, conversation would be made and an invitation given to join us in our worship service. Politely he would decline, stating that they "had to be on their way." More often than not his congregation was far larger than our little congregation, for gambling, at that time, was very prevalent in our county and "poker" was one of the favorite pastimes.

The Indian Creek Church was known for its kind hospitality and friendly atmosphere, plus its good singing; and sing they did! The old gospel songs never sounded quite so good, as they sang with spirit and with feeling.

Dr. and Mrs. John Nesbitt, from the Fifth Avenue Presbyterian Church in New York, came for a visit, staying several days. One night, by light of a lantern, we walked up the hollow with Clay's group for a singing at the home of Ike and Mary Peters. An elderly couple, they were cared for by their daughter Elsie and son Aaron.

Clay's Group sang for over an hour. He and Laura would often sing alone as a duet, then the rest of the group would join in. Dr. Nesbitt was most impressed, and from time to time, as we sang, I watched his face. There was an expression of admiration and love.

Later that night, back at the Cow Creek manse, he solemnly remarked, "Joe, I never heard such singing. Truly, they sang from the heart."

Those singing from the heart were Clay and Laura Thomas, Lela, Henry and Flora Callahan, Viola Marshall, Nancy Callahan, Emma Jean Cole, Forester Robinson, and June Marshall. I feel sure that some day their voices will blend together again with a much larger, celestial choir.

Being single often presented many problems; namely, everyone wanted to match you with his or her favorite available girl or woman. Often three women were in the running at the same time! And, of course, people love to tease you—especially if you are a minister. I was rather shocked by their matchmaking at first, but I soon learned that, when you are teased, it is through affection and love. If the mountain people do not like you, you are completely ignored and left alone. Nothing can be so cruel as to be ignored!

One occasion fueled the fire for many months!

The new road was being built on Cow Creek which meant that there were two alternate routes into Booneville, back through Breathitt County—at least thirty miles around —or over to Indian Creek and through the river—a much, much shorter route. When the river was low, this was the route everyone took.

One day while in Booneville, a member of the Indian Creek Church—young, attractive, and single—asked if I were going home. When I replied that I was, she asked if she might have a ride. Of course I was delighted, and we started merrily on our way.

When we came to where we had to ford the river, evidentially carried away by her presence, I hit the water too quickly and immediately, in the middle of the river, drowned out the engine. There we sat. The car would not start. There was a way to dry out the spark plugs with a cloth, but unfortunately, this was not in my repertoire, and fearful that too many tries would drain the battery of all its power, we sat quietly—embarrassed—in the middle of the river, waiting for the heat of the engine to dry the spark plugs.

Blushing, she turned to me and quickly said, "I just hope that nobody comes by and sees us sitting here like this, stranded in the middle of this river!"

Of course, predestination decreed that *everyone* would be going to Booneville that day and, of course, *everyone* saw us sitting there in the middle of the river. They knew immediately what had happened (it was a common occurrence, especially among inexperienced drivers), and they would stop, asking if there was anything they could do. I would thank them weakly, knowing that, in time, everyone in Owsley County would know of my plight.

For months that was the talk of the area: the fact that the preacher and a young lady had stayed an awful long time in the middle of the river, and, of course, the farther the news travelled, the longer the time we spent in the river together!

One man was to leave an indelible mark upon my ministry through his kindness and his faithfulness.

His name was Brown Minter. An elderly man, in his early years he had attended the Baptist church. He did not attend our little church, but we would often see each other. He was most friendly. He had the small post office at Ricetown. How well I remember, in the early days, seeing a mule, ridden by Robert Caudill, tied to a tree in front of the building. Robert would deliver the mail by mule. Each family had a mailbag, and these would be picked up and taken to the post office, where the mail was received. On the way back the bag would be placed upon the pole. During a snow storm one day, I made movies of the mail being delivered by mule; a beautiful, unusual picture of Kentucky.

In time, Brown started coming to church. There was a special section where he would sit every Sunday, and, once he started, he was faithful. He was most generous in using his truck to pick up those individuals who did not have transportation to church. He would bring them to the service, and afterwards, he would take them home again.

Sunday after Sunday, when everyone had gone and he and I were alone, we would stand outside the church and talk. Nothing serious; nothing in particular; just talk. He was never in a hurry and would gladly have stayed several hours, had I had the time.

His never being in a hurry was indicative of his driving, for he never drove more than ten miles an hour—sometimes only five. I would often be in a hurry, rushing toward Booneville, and get to the bottom of the Margaret Hollon Hill only to find Brown Minter there, travelling at five miles an hour. Unable to pass, his slow driving would delay my arrival for at least twenty to thirty minutes; but, being a good church goer, he was readily forgiven!

Brown was in his eighties and we all knew that he was not well, but he kept going. Finally, the time arrived when it was necessary for him to go to Lexington for an operation. He dreaded the operation, perhaps knowing that at his age the outcome could go either way.

Following his operation, I visited him regularly, but one day a call came from his family that "Brown wants to see Joe." So, early the next morning we drove back to Lexington, Bill Hall, Arvis Trosper, and I.

At St. Joseph's Hospital in the Intensive Care Unit, I went immediately to his bed, but the nurses were working with him and they asked if I would step aside for a few minutes.

Brown refused to let go of my hand, but I explained that I had to go outside for *only* a few minutes. Unable to speak clearly, he muttered a few words.

About thirty minutes later, the nurse came for me and I followed her to his bedside.

He reached for my hand and held it firmly. From memory I recited several Bible verses and then had prayer with him. But he continually kept trying to tell me something—something that I could not understand. The words were there—but unintelligible. He kept shaking his head as though he was saying "No."

Immediately I tried to assure him of the promises of God; of our faith in our Lord Jesus Christ; and, that since he had accepted Christ years ago when he had joined the Baptist Church, he was assured the promises of our Lord. It was then that I finally began to understand what he was trying to tell me.

Slowly I asked, "Brown, did you ever join the church?"

He shook his head, indicating no. All of this time, we had all thought that he belonged to the Baptist Church.

Then I said, "Now, if you can hear me, nod your head yes."

His eyes sparkled and immediately he nodded his head in the affirmative.

Then I knew! I knew what he was trying so hard to say.

"Brown, do you want to accept Christ as your personal Savior? Do you want to be baptized?"

He again nodded his head yes.

I went to a nurse and asked her to get me some water in a paper cup, and quickly returned to his bed. A short prayer was then given, and with tears in my eyes and my voice almost a whisper, I asked God to forgive Brown Minter of his sins and to receive him into His kingdom.

Slowly, with water from the paper cup, I baptized Brown Minter, eighty-six years of age.

For a moment, he held my hand tightly, and through my tear-filled eyes I saw a tired, peaceful face—drawn, but smiling. I remained by his bed holding his hand until he drifted into a deep sleep.

Brown Minter died the next day. We held his funeral on Sunday, at one o'clock, in the little Presbyterian church where, just two weeks before, he had last worshipped.

There are many people that I so well remember from the Indian Creek Church. Bill Bowling, Lula Thomas, Felix and Henry Callahan, Albert Bowling, Beatrice Minter, James Wilder, Marie Marshall, Colson Duff and Kenny Thomas—people of great depth and compassion who, somehow, in their own silent way, gave to our community a special love and, in their own lives, so beautifully exemplified the life of Christ.

Clay Thomas was just such a person. An Elder, he was kind, gentle, and so faithful in the life of our church. Years before, he had walked the four miles to Cow Creek and asked that I not get involved in politics; but, an Elder was running for County Judge and it was my belief that he needed our support—the support of the church—so I slept with a rifle under my bed at night and campaigned fiercely. But our Elder lost. During those years I learned much about religion and politics!

There had been twelve children in the Clay Thomas family and they had always attended our services—even when they had to walk. He took care of the cemetery and, once a year, an offering would be taken for Clay.

I am aware of only one time during my ministry that Clay became quite angry with me! But I thoroughly enjoyed

Children at the Indian Creek Presbyterian Church.

the incident, and, perhaps as one comedian has said, the devil made me do it!

Clay always took up the offering alone at the Indian Creek Church. This was done as I played softly on the piano. He would then walk back up the aisle and, reaching the piano, the congregation would stand and sing "The Doxology."

This was the accepted procedure and, Sunday after Sunday, it never varied; but one Sunday, when the attendance reached more than one hundred, Clay was returning with the offering and had reached the middle of the church. Suddenly I discontinued playing the hymn and started playing, quite loudly, "Here Comes the Bride." Clay stopped in the middle of the aisle holding the collection plate. He was quite upset at my little joke! Clay Thomas, truly, was a leader in our little church!

As we played the various games at C.E. on Thursday nights, little did I know that a boy who attended our youth meetings was later to teach at Westpoint Academy!

In time, those who were young would marry and often move away, and I was to see them only at funerals and on special occasions. Yet, when they did return, there was always a love and joy in remembering, so well, a life once so free, so wonderful, and so simple!

9

Homecoming was a special and an eagerly awaited event in the early days of our church. After finishing high school most of our young people moved on to Cincinnati, Lexington, Louisville or Indiana, but each year Homecoming was the day for returning to the family; to the creek, and to the Cow Creek Presbyterian Church.

For days we cleaned and polished. Tables would be set up in the back room of the church; or, on occasion, if the weather permitted, we ate out in the yard. There was fellowship and laughter, sitting around a long table abundantly laden with fried chicken, ham, chicken and dumplings, pies and cakes, and every conceivable dish prepared by man!

My first Homecoming after coming to Cow Creek was a simple task. We gathered the old, old pictures from the community—some dating back twenty and thirty-five years—and placed them on display in the back room of the church. Gene and Lexene Moore, and Boots and Ralph Reynolds helped me, and after much sorting, pasting, and cutting the displays were arranged on the walls. More than four hundred pictures were glued on red, green, and yellow posterboard.

Special music was provided by Carol and Sharon Gibson; Betty Jean and Kathryn Gilmer; Tom and Betty Niccolls, and William Richards. Nervously, I stood in the large homemade pulpit and delivered the Homecoming address. This was my first Homecoming, but I truly felt that I, too, was a part of Cow Creek!

Though all of the Homecomings were unique and enjoyable, three were to be special to my ministry.

Perhaps the most memorable one was "The Womanless Wedding," which I had seen given many, many times while in North Carolina.

This presentation was both an impossibility and a miracle: Grown men in overalls do not walk down the aisle of a church dressed as bridesmaids! It was simply unbelievable—but it happened!

Evening dresses and wigs were borrowed, and all the necessary items of attire were secured for the making of a first-class wedding; one which Emily Post would have readily given her blessing! Formality was strictly used and everything was according to the best of taste.

Prior to the wedding, the bridal music was never sweeter than that which came from the lips of Rudolph Turner and Ralph Reynolds as they sang "Wedding Bells" and "I'm Throwing Rice at the One I Love." The angels must have been envious!

And then, the wedding march.

Gene Moore—quiet, dignified, the father of two—came timidly down the aisle as the ring bearer—in little short pants.

Quenton Callahan, probably the best and most productive farmer on Cow Creek, dressed in a hemstitched cream lace dress, daintily dropped rose petals from a basket of flowers in the path of the bride.

The crowd was in stitches! The sanctuary was packed, and the laughter was uncontrollable.

The bridesmaids, in formality and in low-cut gowns, with muscles bursting at the seams, graciously "floated" down the rose-strewn aisle. Those "floating" were Clarence Gibson, Earl McIntosh, Wilson Gabbard, and Pleas Turner.

Roscoe Morris—long noted for his unique humor and cheerfulness, weighing two hundred and fifty pounds—made the perfect bride, who swept down the aisle in full splendor. Peter McIntosh, bashful, timid, and blushing—small in stature and in weight—was the groom who waited at the altar. Shelby Moore, in his most articulate voice, was the minister. He performed the ceremony as taken from the *Book of Common Worship*.

Only one item was omitted. The groom refused to kiss the bride!

Following the wedding, the Reverend Albert Tull spoke briefly about the Cow Creek he had known some twenty years before. The Junior Choir, Sharon Gibson, and the Men's Quartet provided the closing music for a perfect evening.

One Homecoming was distinctly different. With great reverence and much dignity, we honored the charter members of our church. A replica of the first Session meeting of the new church—hand painted by an artist in Lexington—was presented to the church and, as each name was called, a red rose was given to each of the original participants who were present. A white carnation was presented to members of the family of the original participants who were deceased.

"The End of a Perfect Day" was sung by Sharon Gibson; and the choir, composed of Lexene Moore, Boots Reynolds, Lois Reynolds, Elsie Morris, Margaret McIntosh, Mary Kennedy, Clarence Gibson, Gene Moore, Kermit Reynolds, Ralph Reynolds, Stanley Reynolds, and Rudolph Turner also sang several hymns.

My constant dream while growing up was to become a second Cecil B. DeMille, and some years later, the opportunity arrived.

Through the Board of National Missions in New York, we borrowed a 16mm movie camera, and production began. Such excitement had never been known!

"A Man and His Valley," written by a young *second* Cecil B. DeMille, was about a man, his valley, and his family—and was thirty minutes in length. Each scene was carefully timed: for financial reasons there could be no retakes. Film was very expensive, and we simply did not have the money for take after take.

Everyone had fun and the entire production was one of great joy! I had but to speak and the actors obediently fell at my feet. Hollywood had come to Cow Creek.

One Sunday afternoon, with camera on tripod, we filmed the final scenes of the men carrying the casket up the long hill to the Wilson Cemetery. The scenery was beautiful. Far down below was the valley and the winding dusty road and, in the distance, the little white church on a hill. Shelby Moore, as the minister, stood over the casket for the committal. Then, there was the sad return down the hill.

Persons from the valley who performed in the movie were Clyde Gabbard, Ethel Turner, Harold Peters, Lexene Moore, Shelby Moore, Dorothy Sue Reynolds, Charles McIntosh, Bobby Wilson, and Will Combs.

Television had not yet reached Cow Creek, nor were there any movie cameras in our area; so, "moviemaking" was a novelty. For weeks, we all waited patiently for the film to be processed and returned. Then, there was the editing—which I did with a pair of scissors, glue, and a 16mm movie projector. The sound was provided by a tape recorder. When the final product was reviewed on screen, our premiere at the

Cow Creek Presbyterian Church equalled Atlanta's "Gone with the Wind."

Everybody loved it! Silently—and in my mind—I took bow after bow after bow for my masterpiece!

There were to be many Homecomings, but these were the most impressive and the most enjoyable!

10

One of the duties of the mission minister is to interpret the work of the Presbyterian Church to supporting churches; so, every so often, an invitation would come and I would travel, either by car or by plane, to speak about our work at Cow Creek. I always enjoyed this task, for it gave me an opportunity to meet, face to face, those who had sent layettes, clothing, or financial gifts to our ministry. During my years at Cow Creek these trips took me to Ohio, Pennsylvania, New York, New Jersey, Tennessee, Indiana, Virginia, West Virginia, Maryland, Michigan, and Massachusetts.

The following article, written by Alice Scott Ross, appeared in the *Springfield Union Newspaper,* Springfield, Massachusetts:

"The Reverend Joe Powlas, of Cow Creek, Booneville, Kentucky, pastor of three churches in Owsley County, came to the Northhampton area this week.

"He came at the invitation of Florence M. Ryder, leader of the Appalachian project, to personally thank the many women who were responsible for the sending of thousands of hand-fashioned garments and gifts for his parishioners.

"Joe Powlas—'Everybody calls me Joe'—is a big, rangy man, six feet four inches tall, and the message he brought from his people well befitted his frame. His warmth and bright humor made the reception being held for him—hosted by Miss Ryder Wednesday at Hearthside (Mrs. Jots' home)—a very special occasion.

"Despite the outside snow and chill—'We have cold weather in Kentucky, too'—there was only friendliness and good cheer inside for the thirty or so women who had come to meet Joe and hear him speak of his Appalachia. There was rapt attention as he shared his concepts of life.

"It was a church 'with a golden roof' that started his ministry. He had come, some twenty-nine years ago, to Owsley County with doubtful hesitancy. As he approached, walking toward his new life, he saw a gleam of gold glistening through the trees.

"The sunlight reflecting off the dusty, corroded tin roof made it a golden gleam, but to Joe it symbolized 'the light of God' and to this day the symbolism remains, although the original roof has long since been replaced.

"Joe spoke of his people and their pride. The county had no industry. Only two percent of the land was tillable. Charity was unacceptable and frowned upon as such. So, a *price* of five cents is always placed on articles sent, which are, therefore, 'bought and sold.'

"Bartering is often resorted to. For example, blackberries were once exchanged for a layette, with both parties experiencing satisfaction.

"And, *Christmas!* This is the most wonderful time of the year. The children all receive gift bags containing new clothing and toys, according to their ages, and an ample supply of apples, oranges and candy. Can you possibly guess what the elderly parishioners cherish most? Lap robes and afghans to tuck around themselves as they sit before their fires—foiling the winter weather.

" 'All clothing sent should be durable and practical; such as work jackets, work shirts, and work pants,' stressed Joe.

152

"Life is changing at Cow Creek just as it is everywhere else. Our young people are leaving to find employment elsewhere. Old arts, such as quilting, are lessening in popularity.

"Food remains pretty much the same—squirrel, fried ham, chicken, biscuits and gravy—always gravy—shuck beans, and cushaw, a variety of squash. Some things never seem to change.

"Reverend Powlas—vibrant, dedicated, filled with a rollicking charm—brought more than just a discussion about his people. He had plain, every day counseling for the group that had come to honor him and receive his thanks.

" 'Be of good cheer,' he said. 'Don't let anyone make you mad. Don't let anyone hurt your feelings. This isn't always easy, but you *can* do it and it will make you strong. And great peace have they which love the Lord.' "

How well I remember these trips! Once en route to the Fifth Avenue Presbyterian Church, in New York, my ego was shattered almost beyond repair. It was a night flight out of Lexington, the skies were dark and turbulent and one wondered if the flight might be canceled. It wasn't. The plane took off on schedule.

Most of the seats were empty. Once during the flight the air became extremely rough. The plane seemed to rock from side to side then, suddenly hitting an air pocket, the plane dropped several feet which, of course, brought immediate fear to everyone on board. In the seat directly in front of me sat an elderly lady, probably around eighty-five or ninety years of age, and it was obvious that she was extremely frightened. She constantly called for the attendant who quickly assured her that everything would be all right; but her words of assurance proved to be of little or no consolation.

Being a minister, I realized that this was an opportunity for my service; so, quickly, I moved into the seat beside her. She looked startled, but said nothing.

Quietly, I began talking; asking questions as to where she had lived; what were her hobbies; did she have any children; had she ever been to Europe; anything to get her mind off the flight.

After about ten minutes, she turned to me and asked, "May I ask a favor of you?"

I was pleased. Perhaps I had been of some help after all, and I was sure that she was going to ask me to offer a word of prayer during this difficult time.

"Sure," I answered. "Anything."

She looked me straight in the eye. "PLEASE *shut up!*"

Stunned, my ego smashed, I returned quickly to my seat and sat in silence for the rest of the flight.

There was a speaking engagement in Cincinnati, at the College Hill Presbyterian Church. Two weeks earlier, a down payment had been made on a new Chevrolet automobile; so, as I travelled on Highway 75 in my brand-new car, there was a feeling of security and happiness, something one never experiences in the older vehicles. No more recapped tires to blow out. No more breakdowns! But, at a gas station this side of Newport, my new car suddenly caught fire—the wiring in the dashboard—and I stood there, frantically, not believing that this was happening to me! Luckily, an attendant had enough sense to grab a fire extinguisher and put the fire out. A wrecker had to be called. Joe Powlas in all his glory, in his brand-new car, arrived in Cincinnati behind a tow truck, heading for a Chevrolet garage.

A telephone call was made to Billy Bruce Peters, who had been at Cow Creek years before, and I informed him of my situation. Within a few minutes he was there, and we went to his Newport home for supper. The program at the church was scheduled to begin at 7 p.m., so I reminded Billy Bruce that we should be there on time.

"But, I'm not sure I know just where the College Hill Presbyterian Church is," said Billy Bruce.

"It's on Hamilton Avenue," I answered.

"I'm not sure I know where Hamilton Avenue is," he replied. "Oh, wait. Yes I do! I know *exactly* where it is."

With great skill, he drove like a demon, across the bridge leading into Cincinnati, down eight or ten streets and, finally, with a screeching halt, stopped the car in front of a large stone church.

"Why don't you come in with me?" I asked.

"Nope! Not me. I'm not dressed. I'll stay right here until you get back."

Since I had never been there before I had no idea what the church looked like. There was no sign at the side entrance but Billy Bruce seemed to know what he was doing, so I trusted his judgment. I ran quickly to the door and stepped inside. People in an adjoining room were talking and I presumed that they were worried about my late arrival; so I opened the door and said apologetically, "I'm sorry that I am late!" Immediately nuns and priests, too numerous to count, looked at me with bewilderment and shock! A strange quietness settled upon the room. I raised my hand in greeting, smiled, and quickly retreated back to the car and Billy Bruce.

"Boy, that was a short meeting," he stammered.

"I think it would be best if we stopped at a filling station and asked for directions."

We did and I finally made the meeting, but everyone at the College Hill Presbyterian Church found it amusing that my first stop had been at a Roman Catholic Church.

An unknown policeman in Pittsburgh, Pennsylvania, will always be the recipient of my deepest gratitude and appreciation.

There had been a speaking engagement at the Women's Home and Foreign Missionary Society at the First Presbyterian Church, on Sixth Avenue. A wonderful group, these ladies had supported most generously our work at Cow Creek and I felt honored to be with them that afternoon.

However, my lodging was in Washington, about twenty miles away. Someway, somehow—although directions had been carefully given—I got lost in the madness of the five p.m. traffic. Slowly and carefully, the car was driven to the outside lane, then stopped on the curb.

As I sat there, confused, frustrated and a little sad, a policeman on a motorcycle came toward me. He looked stern, tired, as though he had already had a most tiring day. Immediately I began to wonder what a traffic ticket would cost in Pittsburgh.

"What's the problem?" he asked kindly.

"It looks so simple, here on the map; but once I get out there in the traffic, the simplicity is lost. I am trying to get down to Washington, but I am hopelessly lost! Just . . . plain . . . lost," my words were absorbed in the roar of the heavy traffic.

He looked like a mother hen about to draw her little chicks to safety.

"Go down about one-half mile; turn left, be sure you stay in the middle lane until you are almost to the intersection, then turn . . ." But there was already confusion in my mind and he conjectured this just by the look on my face.

"I tell you what let's do," he smiled. "You just follow me and when we get to the road you want, I'll wave and you just go on past me."

And so, Joe Powlas, from Cow Creek, Kentucky, had a police escort through Pittsburgh, Pennsylvania, for at least five miles. No ticket, but an escort! A Presbyterian minister was truly grateful to a policeman who had gone out of his way to show kindness, concern, and compassion that day; and that night, on my knees, I asked God to give that policeman a double blessing!

My most unusual happening occurred at a speaking engagement at the Church of the Covenant, in Washington, Pennsylvania.

The Women's Association Dinner was scheduled for six p.m. My plan was to arrive at the home of Lew and Peg Hays at about four p.m., where I would rest, shower, dress and be at the church about five forty-five.

Everything went wrong. The speed limit had been lowered from seventy to fifty-five nationwide, and there were state police everywhere, strictly enforcing the new law, and to make matters worse, my departure from Cow Creek had been later than expected.

Driving frantically, I realized that there was no way I could arrive at the Hays home by four o'clock. I would even be lucky to get to the church by six.

Glancing down at the gasoline gauge at about five forty-five I discovered that it was on empty and I still had about fifteen miles to go. Never had a minister felt such frustration, such despair. Then I spotted an off-brand gasoline station off the road, just over the hill. I really preferred the well-known brands for, with credit cards, my gasoline could be charged; but, this was an emergency and I had no choice. So, hurriedly, a tired and aggravated minister pulled off the main road and drove down to the little off-brand station.

The attendant was a boy about sixteen years of age, who chewed gum and had a large black radio playing full blast. He sang and kept time with the music as he put five dollars worth of gas into my car. The loudness of his radio equalled the roaring of a jet plane engine and the music was without intelligence.

I asked if I might use the bathroom to change clothes. "Sure," he said. "Make yourself at home. It's at the back of the building."

So I pulled my car away from the gas tanks, got my clothing, and entered into the dirtiest, filthiest bathroom I had ever seen—or smelled. Quickly, I put on a new shirt, the dry-cleaned suit, tied my tie, then reached for the metal door, ready to depart. The handle came off in my hand! Nervously, I tried to put the handle back on the shaft, but the shaft went in the opposite direction, past my reach; so there I stood, a grown man, all dressed to speak, with the door handle in my hand!

One cannot imagine my anguish!

I banged, I screamed, I yelled, but all that could be heard was the rock and roll music at full blast! I even took off my shoe and banged on the metal door, but no one could hear. No one.

Slowly, my tired, lanky frame sat down on the dirty commode. What would I do? How long would I be there? Would the boy check the bathroom before locking up for the night?

Ten minutes later, my salvation arrived when a little old man wanted in just as badly as I wanted out. There was a knock on the door; I quickly told him to retrieve the other piece of the door handle, which he did; then, thankfully, we both fulfilled our destinies.

I arrived at the Church of The Covenant about an hour late; but, whereas the supper was missed, I still had time for the program where I spoke of our ministry in the hills of Kentucky.

One of the greatest enjoyments of my speaking engagements was in meeting individuals with whom I had corresponded for many years.

I don't remember exactly when I first learned of Barbara Campbell. In a way it seems that we always knew one another. Perhaps it was through the New York Avenue Presbyterian Church in Washington, D.C.—or it could have been through the D.A.R. School of Crossnore, down in North Carolina, which she also supported. Someway, somehow she secured my name and our friendship began.

Every so often a package of used clothing would arrive. One always knew her boxes, intricately tied with twine, wrapped hundreds of times around the box. It must have taken hours to secure them. Then, once or twice a year, a small check would come with the apology that she wished more could be shared. I later learned that she was more than generous with everyone. Once she wrote of reading about a person in the newspaper and a check had been sent to him. Another time she wrote about sharing with a person she had seen on television. She had compassion for everyone, and I understand, she literally gave away every penny that she possessed.

One year while in Washington, the host suggested several places I might visit during some free time. It took me only a second to decide—Wyoming Apartments, 2022 Columbia Road. The call was made, and at long last I met Barbara Campbell. I stood in excitement as she entered the lobby. Strange how preconceived images lock within the mind. Through the years I had pictured Barbara Campbell to be a large, rotund, redheaded person. Instead, she was tall, stately, quiet, and had a timid smile.

Sometime later the invitation came to speak at the Women's Association of the New York Avenue Presbyterian Church and we met again. Following the meeting, she remained for a few minutes and asked me many questions about Cow Creek and about my work.

Shy, quiet, withdrawn—there was an eloquence about her that I could never forget, a strange beauty that haunted me long after we parted.

Those two brief meetings left an indelible mark upon me. Thin, frail, soft-spoken, hesitating before speaking, I found in her the essence of goodness and a quality of life to which we all aspire.

When the letter arrived with news of her death—caused by complications due to malnutrition—I knew both sorrow and joy. My sorrow was caused by realizing that the church had lost such a wonderful person. My joy was in knowing that she truly was one of the wealthiest persons I had ever known! Her wealth consisted of that which is really important. Her treasures were not of this earth and she found, so beautifully, the secret of life. Through Christian love she gave of herself without reservation. She gave all that she had, to the poor; to the needy; to starving animals; to strangers; to the homeless; to hungry children in foreign lands; and to the church.

She was truly one of the most beautiful persons I have ever known. I thank God that, in my lifetime, I was privileged to meet so great a person.

11

The ministry is a calling of many facets and, in every ministry, there is the joy of working with young people. A special part of my life belonged to the young people of the Cow Creek and of the Indian Creek churches.

The boys and girls over fourteen years of age came in once a week on Friday nights for Christian Endeavor or C.E. Some walked, but most came by way of the Blue Goose. Through the years we were to have our ghost story outings, climbing to the top of a mountain in total darkness to tell scary tales in some lonely deserted cemetery; scavenger hunts up and down the creek finding frogs and year old calendars; or else we played Flying Dutchman and Snatch the Bacon in the churchyard. There was laughter, gaiety, wonderful Christian fellowship as we ran and played, or as we bowed and worshipped.

There was an old Dodge bus given to our ministry, and this immediately became known to our young people as the Blue Goose. The Blue Goose was used for church services and for the youth work. Ironically, though, we pushed it more than we rode. When started, it would dramatically cough and sputter then, in all probability, the motor would completely die. One night, on Indian Creek, while taking the young people home from a youth meeting, the Blue Goose gave a strange choking sound then promptly quit.

In complete darkness, we all walked the four and one-half miles home. Since it was common for the Cow Creek kids to attend the Indian Creek meetings and vice versa, there were about ten Cow Creek kids with me that night.

It was cold, it was dark, and there was a light rain; but, triumphantly, we sang all the way back to the Cow Creek manse. We sang "Amazing Grace," "Froggy Went a Courting," "Shall We Gather at the River," "Sixteen Tons," "The Old Rugged Cross," and "The Yellow Rose of Texas." Passing Brown Minter's, we sang as loudly as we could.

"Maybe he will have mercy on us and come out and take us home," one of the kids remarked, tired from walking. The remark was fruitless. No truck appeared so we continued walking.

A new DCE had come to Booneville and I was interested in making a hit with her. My plan (and this seemed to be the general plan which was commonly used by most of the local boys) was that we would all go up to the cemetery behind James Wilson's and tell ghost stories. Then the girls, scared to death, would hang on to the boys coming back down the hill. The new DCE would hang on to Joe Powlas. The idea was infallible. To make the plan more realistic Earl and I went up to the cemetery a day early, taking a pair of pants, some shoes and a coat. These were stuffed, forming a dummy. Since no head could be made, we simply put leaves and limbs over that part of the body. The feet, protruding from the stuffed pants and coat, looked very real. We prided ourselves on our ability. When Friday night came, we would both have us a girl! Nothing could go wrong!

But something *did* go wrong—very much so—in more ways than one. First, the Blue Goose took a stubborn spell and, even with all of our pushing, she absolutely refused to start.

"Push harder," we cried to the boys and girls behind the bus. "Push harder and maybe, this time, she will start."

She refused.

Taking Earl to the side, I calmly stated, "Earl, next week will be just as good. We'll get someone to work on the carburetor, and we will have our ghost stories next Friday."

So, we went up to the church and played Flying Dutchman and Snatch the Bacon, had our devotions, and I took the kids home in the car—making several trips, of course.

At that time Owsley County was going through a crisis. The sheriff and his deputy had been murdered at the mouth of Cow Creek several weeks before, and there had been a killing over on Buffalo; so, the tension was quite high.

I am told that, late one evening of the following week, one of the local farmers went to round up his cows. Ordinarily, he did not go through the cemetery but took another route. That night, however, his wife had made plans to go to a meeting, so she had asked him to hurry. He took the shortcut through the cemetery. As he walked hurriedly past the graves, to his horror he looked down and saw the body of a man at the foot of a grave. The report is that he ran to the home of a neighbor at the bottom of the hill on the other side.

"Clay, come quickly," he yelled. "Someone has been murdered up there in the cemetery. The blow flies are already working on him."

So, Clay and his sons grabbed several shotguns and rifles, and they all hurried back up to the cemetery.

Cautiously, the body was approached. Taking the butts of their guns, they slowly turned the corpse over—only to find the dummy!

The simple remark was made, "Joe Powlas has been here."

The farmer who had found the body bent over and took

the shoes—my good shoes—and said, "Well, at least I will get me a good pair of shoes out of this."

We never told the ghost stories that week and, before the opportunity availed itself again, the DCE was gone.

Three women who came from Washington, Pennsylvania, were quite special: Mildred McMahon, Louise Stiles and Melina Campbell! Year after year they came down with their youth groups, conducting our Vacation Bible Schools, working with youth projects, and becoming a part of the fellowship of our community. Everybody loved them, for they truly were great!

I am sure the devil made me do it. One day I took a reel-to-reel tape recorder and recorded perfect silence the first thirty minutes, then an occasional "ah" and a moan, then a cough, then heavy breathing. This lasted about ten minutes. While the three women were swimming at the river, the tape recorder had been taken upstairs to their bedroom in the manse and hidden under one of the beds.

That night after we had completed our games the adults sat around and talked. Finally Melina said (and this brought joy to my heart!), "Don't you think it is about time that we all went to bed. I'm tired."

I made some weak excuse about checking the fan upstairs —I went upstairs hurriedly, plugged the tape recorder in, then bade them all good night.

There was no intention of going out to Clyde's right at that moment. I waited patiently outside in the darkness by the side of the manse. In about twenty minutes the lights upstairs went out. I waited and waited and nothing happened. I began to get worried. Perhaps I had failed to set the buttons correctly. Maybe the tape recorder had not been turned on. Then it happened! Screams came forth that could be heard for four miles up the creek! I have never heard such screams in all of my life. The lights came on—first in their bedroom, then throughout the manse one room at a time. The screaming continued even louder than before, and I could tell that pure pandemonium had broken loose in the manse.

I walked quickly out to Clyde's and silently went upstairs to bed; but it was a long, long time before I was able to sleep, for the bed shook from laughter.

Telling ghost stories at the top of the mountain was a specialty in the early years. The young people always looked forward to going; but, as the years progressed, the possibility of being bitten by either a rattlesnake or copperhead became quite serious. So, in time, this trek up the dark mountain was discontinued altogether.

Tales were told of Ida Caudill, over on Buffalo, finding a copperhead in her oven as she prepared supper; of Arvis Trosper sitting on the couch in his living room and seeing a copperhead sticking his head out between the cushions; of Willie Cooper carrying a stack of tobacco sticks on his shoulder from one end of the field to the other. When the sticks were dropped to the ground a large copperhead slithered at his feet. Had the snake bitten Willie on the neck there is little chance that he would have survived! We also heard about a woman over on Meadow Creek who took in her washing one day only to discover in the bottom of her clothes basket a large forty-eight inch copperhead. Some of the tales became quite frightening. Fearful lest some young person—or one Joe Powlas—might be bitten, we discontinued going to the hilltop cemeteries in the dark. Still, the ghost stories continued, either in the graveyard (Where the next day we would always discover we had a bumper crop of chiggers!) or else in the back room of the church, where we often ended up with splinters.

One method we used was to seat the young people on the floor in a circle, place one lit candle in the middle of the circle, then tell ghost stories that had accumulated through the years. Though often told and repeated, the kids always seemed to enjoy the retelling. Every so often frightened whispers and screams would still be heard.

The climax always came with "the passing of the body." Though sometimes *too* mature for the younger folks, the young people insisted that it be shared with our youth group guests.

My story usually began with the statement that Dick Searcy, the local mortician, was a good friend of mine. Knowing that we were going to be telling ghost stories that night, I had gone to the funeral home that day and asked Dick if he might help me with my story telling. He obliged me by stating that there had been a horrible automobile accident that day and one of the bodies had been so badly mangled and crushed that it was impossible to embalm it, but he would gladly loan me some of the *pieces of the body* to be used while telling our ghost stories.

The lone candle would be extinguished and then, in total darkness, a piece of the body would be passed from person to person, starting with me. As soon as that piece (which would often be thrown to the floor by some frightened or squeamish girl, necessitating a search in the darkness before continuing the story) was returned to me, another piece would be placed into the person's hands sitting next to me.

We started off with a shirt. No big deal! Then a shoe. Still no reaction—only giggles. Then a wig, dampened with water, which *immediately* brought a few groans. The story began to become real.

Then I would pass around a small peeled peach—for an eyeball. This produced more than a few screams.

Balloons, filled with water and greased with Vaseline,

were then passed around and thought to be intestines, producing more groans and screams.

The final item, which was the most frightening, was a large, cold, piece of meat, which might lead one to believe it was a piece of flesh from the dead man's body. All this in total darkness!

Our local kids had sat through these happenings many times, so the real thrill came when some unsuspecting youth group from Akron, Cincinnati, Knoxville, McLean, or Penfield came, unaware of what was about to happen!

C.E. was the big event of the week. The young people would often walk several miles, getting to the manse about three or four o'clock in the afternoon. Whereas we usually had about twenty to twenty-five at a meeting, occasionally there would be as many as sixty or seventy. The usual format was games or activities such as Flying Dutchman or, in the winter, the ChoCho game, or the numbers game. In time, movies would be secured and these also would be shown. A few of the adults on Cow Creek would come to the meeting but remain outside in the car. Then, when the movies began, they would come in silently and watch the movie along with the young people. Devotions were important. We always ended our get-togethers with scripture, meditation, and a prayer.

Cow Creek was once asked to be host to a two-county Youth Rally, sponsored by the Presbyterian Church. Our only responsibility was to take charge of the activities and provide Kool-Aid for the estimated one hundred and fifty to two hundred young people who would be present.

We looked forward to the day in great anticipation and organized for the occasion. First, a large washtub was secured and scrubbed spotlessly clean. The girls were assign-

167

ed the task of making the Kool-Aid, and the boys would carry the tub up to the church when it was ready.

Everything was going according to schedule. I went into the manse to check on the girls, who had carefully mixed the sugar and the store-bought packages of Kool-Aid. The taste was simply delicious. The girls smiled, proud of a task well done.

As the boys were bringing the tub up to the back room about an hour later, I noticed a strange consistency in the Kool-Aid. There were little white specks floating around on the top!

When I questioned the girls they readily admitted what had happened. That particular day, at the little grocery store on Cow Creek, free samples of Jergens lotion were being distributed; and the boys, just to aggravate the girls, put four bottles of Jergens lotion into the tub of Kool-Aid.

There was no money for additional sugar and Kool-Aid, nor was there time to remake it if we'd had the money. So, smiling weakly, we started dipping out the liquid to the long line of kids who eagerly awaited their refreshments!

Incredible as it may seem, no one said anything about the taste, every drop was consumed and, frankly, it actually tasted quite good!

Strange how a person remembers insignificant bits of life, while other items of far greater importance are discarded and not retained by the mind.

Why should I remember that day at the manse when Earl McIntosh and Billy Bruce Peters made a bet on which one of them could consume the most eggs?

Eggs become quite plentiful in the spring. Whenever I visited a home, invariably a dozen eggs would be placed in my hands when leaving; so, in time, I had accumulated eight to ten dozen eggs in my refrigerator.

One day, the question was asked, "What in the world am I going to do with all these eggs?"

Billy Bruce quickly remarked, "Why not have an egg-swallowing contest? The person who swallows the most eggs before throwing up will be declared the winner!"

We'd had shooting contests on the creek, where the men vied to see who could kill the most squirrels in a season, but I had never even heard of an egg-swallowing contest.

Word about this contest went out and, several days later, Billy Bruce, Earl IcIntosh, and the young people gathered at the manse for the event.

Earl broke the first egg and quickly swallowed it. Billy Bruce followed in similar fashion. The first five eggs seemed to go down rather easily for both contestants. Then the boys paused for several minutes before continuing.

Earl swallowed his sixth egg. Billy Bruce followed with his sixth egg. Earl cracked the shell on his seventh egg, then quickly swallowed it. Billy Bruce was determined to stay abreast—though I noticed he seemed to be getting a little white around the eyes.

The rules of the game stated that there would be no stopping. The eggs had to be swallowed in sequence. On the tenth egg, I noticed that Earl seemed just a little nauseated, but he continued. Billy Bruce closed his eyes and swallowed his tenth egg.

The crowd stood in awed attention. No one made a sound. On the table out in the yard was a pan of eggs. Each boy stood to be a hero, though there was a price to be paid.

Earl slowly and rather painfully downed his twelfth egg. We could tell he was getting sick, but he still managed to smile, ever so weakly.

Billy Bruce put the twelfth egg in his mouth and, as though pushing with all his strength, he swallowed it.

There was deadly silence.

Earl picked up his thirteenth egg, closed his eyes, and, with the muscles of a woodsman and farmer, swallowed the egg.

Billy Bruce reached for another egg.

Momentarily, it seemed that he turned green. Then, abruptly, he turned and ran for the creek.

Earl was the victor—winning out on the thirteenth egg!

He was a handsome youth with a most wonderful personality, perhaps fifteen or sixteen years of age. Quite naturally, all of the girls were immediately drawn to him. He had everything—a Charles Atlas physique, a charming smile, an unusually high intelligence, and the ability to draw girls like honey draws flies. The girl he would choose each week lived on "Cloud Nine," and became the envy of all her companions.

This, of course, drew stern consternation from the local boys. They always seemed to come in second. *If* one of the local boys were lucky enough to catch on with the most beautiful girl from a visiting youth group, he would immediately get left behind when the girl discovered "Prince Charming!"

Little by little the local boys built up their resentment. And, though quiet and peaceful, I knew that their anger was slowly mounting, and it was just a matter of time before it would explode.

Shortly thereafter it exploded—but not in any manner I had ever visualized.

This boy had his "pick of the litter" during the months of June and July. Just being sweet and kind, he never exploited his magnetism, and this casual attitude infuriated the local boys even more. He did absolutely nothing special to attract the girls. They simply came running after him and fell willingly at his feet!

170

The last youth group for the summer was scheduled for August. I knew the local boys were doing a lot of whispering amongst themselves, but I had no idea what they were planning. Still, my inner senses warned me that something was coming.

When the last group arrived, true to form, the girls were immediately drawn to Prince Charming. Without so much as a wink he gathered them under his wing as a mother hen would with her chicks. This was the case on Sunday, Monday, and Tuesday, but on Wednesday he was ignored *completely!*

Every time he walked up to a girl and smiled, she would turn and walk away without speaking, leaving him alone and thoroughly puzzled.

I was just as puzzled as he. I could not help but wonder what had happened, nor did I know what strategy the local boys used but, whatever it was, it worked!

"What's wrong, Joe?" he asked me. "What have I done?" There was no answer to his question.

For the first time in a long time, the local boys were smiling and walking around with attractive and beautiful girls from the Pennsylvania youth group clinging to their arms. They had finally received the attention that had long been denied them—and they loved every moment!

Personally I was dying from curiosity, so I approached one of the counsellors and asked if she knew what had happened. "No I don't," she said. "But, I *will* find out!" With these words she hurried off to the Summer White House, and she was back in fifteen minutes—breathless.

"Joe," she spoke in almost a whisper. "That poor boy has a horrible disease. You know . . ." she paused for a second, "one of those *sexual* diseases."

So, *that* was the strategy! *That* was their plan. The local boys had spread the rumor that "Prince Charming" had syphilis, gonorrhea or some other dreaded disease. There was absolutely no truth to the rumor, but the "strategy" had worked for the local boys—even *better* than they had hoped.

Even though I thoroughly, carefully, and honestly explained to the girls that the "rumor" was not true, the damage had already been done. Prince Charming finished out the summer alone and rejected!

I thoroughly reprimanded the local boys and secured their solemn promise that never again would they tell such a tale; and so far as I know, they never did!

One summer Sue Brown and a group of young people came to Cow Creek from the Forty-third Avenue Presbyterian Church of Gary, Indiana. They all had a great visit. When the day for departure came, one boy came up on the hill with a fruit jar filled with water.

"Joe, if you don't mind, I am taking this water back to the baptismal fount in our church. I am going to be baptized next Sunday, and I want to be sprinkled with Cow Creek water!"

Mind? On the contrary—I felt honored. I had never been so pleased!

There were three station wagons loaded up for the return trip to Gary. It was a Saturday morning and, after saying good-bye, one carload asked Sue if they might—just for a few minutes—go back to Indian Creek to say good-bye to Shirley Wilder, Darryl and Dale. "Yes," was the reply. "But only for a minute."

Fifteen minutes passed and the kids had not returned.

"Sue," came the plea from the second wagon, "let us go over and see what is wrong. They may have had a flat tire. We would also like to say good-bye to the Wilders."

Sue agreed.

Thirty minutes passed and neither station wagon had returned.

172

So, in desperation, Sue and her wagon took off to Indian Creek.

About an hour later all three wagons pulled up on the hill. Then, with a round of handshaking and a few tears, the three wagons, loaded with young people and one jar of creek water, headed back to Gary, Indiana.

The young people from the Lewinsville Presbyterian Church of McLean, Virginia, came to Cow Creek during many summers. They conducted our Vacation Bible School for us in the early days. They also installed a 2,000 volume library in the little Indian Creek Grammar School. Through their efforts enough TV books were collected to purchase a church van for the Cow Creek Church. Now, my car could be parked for awhile. Prior to getting the van I used my car for picking people up and bringing them to church on Sunday. We rejoiced in our good fortune.

Lew and Peg Hays from the Church of the Covenant, and Dale Campbell, from Washington, Pennsylvania, were also instrumental in our busy and active summers. Through their direction and expertise, Vacation Bible Schools were held, softball games became an art, and the valley rang with laughter and with gaiety.

During the later years, our Vacation Bible Schools were conducted by the Westminster Presbyterian Church, from Akron, Ohio. They came, bringing their own materials and sharing so beautifully the love of Christ with our own people. Our young people and children looked forward to this fellowship and this time of learning, and the memories lingered from one year until the next.

So, the youth groups came from Tennessee, Indiana, Ohio, New York, Pennsylvania, Michigan, Massachusetts, New Jersey, and Kansas.

David Smith, holding rattlesnake killed on Cow Creek.

I vividly remember one group from Michigan, and two incidents that happened which were rather unusual.

This group's project was to build an outdoor toilet. It was to be for the girls—a two-seater. Much drawing and planning went into the project. (Engineers *always* have numerous drawings, with pages and pages of detail—even for a john!)

A decision was made to dig the hole exceptionally deep, using dynamite to expedite the digging. Unaware of the fine art of placing dynamite, Arvis and I placed *two* sticks under a large rock, presuming that the pressure would go down. (*one-half* of a stick would have been more than sufficient). The big moment came. Everyone was excited. They all wanted to witness the dynamite "going off."

"This is dangerous," I warned. "Please stand back." They all moved back several hundred feet.

"Better play it safe," I added. "Better move back some more." The young people all heeded my command.

Arvis struck the match and lit the fuse, and we both ran as fast as our legs would carry us to join the others.

When the "boom" came, it was more than just a boom. In fact, it showered the entire ball field with rocks and debris that were thrown in all directions—far beyond our region of shelter. Rocks hit the top of the Summer White House, car tops, and young people alike. Luckily—thank the Lord—no one was seriously injured. One boy was cut on the wrist by a falling stone, necessitating his being taken to the emergency room of the Good Samaritan Hospital in Lexington.

The other incident concerned the same church—First Presbyterian Church of Ann Arbor, Michigan—but with a different group of young people, and several years later.

Shootings, at times, become rather common in Owsley County. One evening after a delightful visit with Everett and Chaney Byrd, and a church service up on Sextons Creek, the group returned as usual to the Summer White House. In the dark, one of the boys accidentally took hold of a frayed electrical wire and received quite a shock. A diabetic, he became rather upset and momentarily emotionally unstable. This lasted for just a few minutes, and in time, he was all right.

Since he was on medication, a call was placed to Dr. Bob Cornett in Jackson, seeking his advice. His diagnosis was that, in all probability, the boy would be all right but to play it safe we should take him to the emergency room at the Good Samaritan Hospital in Lexington for a complete check-up.

Time was of the utmost importance, and since money was no problem, I went to the manse and called for an ambulance, stating simply that we wanted to take one of our young people to an emergency room at a hospital in Lexington.

"Has he been in a wreck?" the attendant asked.

"No," I replied. "He has been shocked."

We waited and waited for the ambulance. Strange that it should take so long. When the ambulance finally arrived, it was being escorted by the local sheriff and several deputies with their police lights flashing. They jumped out of their cars and ran over to me asking where the victim was.

"Sitting over there," I replied calmly, and pointed to the injured boy.

"Where was he shot?" the sheriff asked.

Then I understood immediately, "Shot? He wasn't *shot!* He was *shocked!*"

The ambulance driver had refused to come without the sheriff who, at the time of the call, was over on Buffalo investigating a disturbance.

As they placed the boy in the ambulance with one of the adult advisors, I shouted to the advisor, "Go on with him. I will see that the kids are settled, then I will come and get you both."

The ambulance pulled out with its lights flashing. The local law returned to Booneville. I separated the boys and the girls, taking the girls over to the manse and leaving the boys at the Summer White House.

On the Mountain Parkway I suddenly realized that there were five hospitals in Lexington and I had no idea to which one they would be taking him; so, quickly, the accelerator was pressed to the floor with the hope that I might catch up with the ambulance. In all probability, my speed exceeded eighty-five to ninety miles an hour!

Then it happened! Suddenly, from out of the darkness there appeared the flashing blue light of the state patrol. Obediently, I slowed down and pulled over to the side of the road.

"You know you were flying, don't you?" remarked the officer.

My voice was calm, more out of irritation than of anger.

"Officer, I was just trying to catch up with an ambulance. One of our kids is being rushed to the hospital and I don't know to which hospital they are taking him."

"Is your wife with him?" he asked.

"She's not my wife," I paused, without actually thinking what I was saying. "She's not my wife. No, we are not married."

"Oh," he replied, shocked.

"Listen, I'm a Presbyterian minister. Just give me a ticket and let me go on."

"Oh . . . oh," were his only remarks. "Oh?" he repeated, and then he smiled and smiled and smiled. Without saying a word he motioned with his hand for me to go on. I pulled the car back into the road and headed for Lexington. Why had he been so inquisitive? Why had my words not been coherent? As I continued on to Lexington, the thought occurred to me that, perhaps, the officer had been a Presbyterian!

But, then again, perhaps it would have been better had he been a Baptist!

The most beautiful prayer I ever heard was *not* given in the Crossnore, North Carolina Presbyterian Church *nor* at the Louisville Theological Seminary, *nor* was it prayed by a minister or by a professor. The prayer was given one night at the close of our C.E. at the Cow Creek Presbyterian Church by Alpha McIntosh who, at the time, was probably about sixteen years of age.

On the spur of the moment, I had turned to Alpha. "Alpha, would you give the prayer for us this evening?" To my knowledge she had never prayed in public before, so her consent surprised me.

"Sure," she answered, stood up and delivered the most beautiful prayer that I have ever heard. It was a prayer of pure beauty; a prayer of great depth; and a prayer of sincerity; but more, it was a prayer of dedication and of love. She prayed from her heart and from her soul. We could actually feel the presence of the Holy Spirit as the words left her lips. No other prayer in my ministry has ever touched me so much as did the prayer that night, given by one of our own young people.

Softball became a way of life at Cow Creek. The boys played softball, and the men played softball. Sunday afternoons were always devoted to playing this exciting and fascinating game, weather permitting.

The Cow Creek Church took their softball very seriously. They played to win. Only those individuals who could hit home runs or make spectacular catches were entitled to play on the Cow Creek team. This became the goal of every young boy on the creek—to play on the church team!

It also became the goal of every other team within the

area to beat the Cow Creek team—but this was rarely accomplished!

Three of our boys stand out most vividly in my softball memories.

Tommy Gabbard, to my knowledge, was the best all-around player we ever had. He was the most versatile; the best hitter; the best runner; and the best at shortstop, where no ball ever got past his glove.

Each game became psychological. When we would play among ourselves, Tommy's team always won! *Always.* Even though I often gave him the worst players—stacking the deck against him—*his* team won. It became weird! He *never* lost! When you played *against* Tommy Gabbard, you automatically lost. It seemed he would and could play the entire field by himself, if need be!

Danny Callahan was quiet and reserved. He played a powerful game of softball; and he, too, seemed to always be on the winning team—though he came on the scene several years later than Tommy. Danny was a wonderful, devoted Christian lad. I will never forget the Sunday we had an eight inch snow. The services had been canceled, but I found Danny's footprints in the deep snow, where he had walked up the hill hoping to attend church.

Mikey Thomas, from Indian Creek, could make more spectacular catches than any human being who ever lived. He even caught the impossible! Balls would be hit to an area where Mikey was just too far away to do anything about it but, someway, somehow, the ball always ended up in his glove. He, too, was truly spectacular.

The one goal in life shared both by the visiting teams and the surrounding teams was to beat Cow Creek. Sure, there were occasions when we lost, but ninety-eight percent of the time the victory was ours.

A youth group once came from Kansas City and participated in the traditional Sunday evening softball game—Cow Creek vs. Kansas City. It was only the fifth inning, and the game had reached the preposterous score of 33 to 4, with Cow Creek leading.

The visiting counsellor called time and his youth group went into a huddle. When they emerged they were all smiling.

They changed pitchers! Not only was it a different pitcher—it was a girl!

Now back in those days, no girl had ever played on the Cow Creek team. Nor do I ever remember a girl playing in any game. Softball was a game to be taken seriously and only the best, the most experienced players were qualified to play.

But they had changed pitchers. And the pitcher who walked out to the pitcher's mound that day was a girl, wearing shorts—short shorts—*much* shorter than the girls ordinarily wore! They were *extremely* short!

She was a beautiful girl; tall and slender, and more attractive than any Hollywood starlet. She smiled, and threw the ball.

Our boys couldn't hit a thing.

They swung at the balls—and missed. They swung at the strikes—and missed.

She just smiled and continued to throw, wiggling her hips just a little bit every time she delivered the ball.

The Cow Creek team literally went to pieces, and they almost lost the game. Whereas in the fifth inning the score had been 33 to 4, at the conclusion of the game, we had won by only two runs—33 to 31!

12

A group came to Cow Creek one summer that was certainly different from the clans that usually arrived. They were very polite, most active in their church, and they all had wonderful personalities. But every person in the group weighed—and this is a conservative guess—over two hundred pounds! Not one of the group was thin! I am not sure if this is a characteristic indicative of their area or town but, should the opportunity ever present itself, I hope to visit their church and see for myself!

Toby, our horse, absolutely refused to let any of them get on his back and ride. One afternoon one of the smaller members of the group tried and tried, unsuccessfully, to mount Toby, but he would not stand still. The boy, apologetically, hugged the horse and murmured, "I understand!"

Each day at two p.m. there was swimming at the river. At that time we were going into the water down behind Carl Stepp's. The river was deeper there, the banks were steeper, but we were able to drive directly to the swimming hole with no walking.

All twenty members of the group went in swimming. The day was hot, the water was most refreshing, and they welcomed a good country swim!

While everyone was in swimming, there was a sudden

downpour. It did not last very long, but, as a result, the banks became wet and extremely slippery. The place where the swimmers had entered the river had become an impossible spot from which to exit.

As they attempted to come out of the river, more water was dripped onto the bank, making it more slippery than ever.

Try as they would the swimmers could not get up the bank! Arvis and I had not gone in that day. We tried to give them a hand, but we simply did not have the leverage—nor the strength—to pull them out.

One of the large swimmers would come running out of the water, get half-way up the bank then slide back into the river. Had the youth group been skinny, or even of average weight, this would not have been funny at all, but since they were all extremely fat, it was hilarious! They laughed as hard as Arvis and I . . . We all laughed . . .

We sat down and laughed . . . They laughed as, one by one, they would slide back into the river. They even formed a line, hoping that, together, they could push at least one person out of the river and up the bank, but, alas, this only proved more hilarious!

We finally solved our problem by having them all walk downstream in the river for about a half mile to where the banks were sloped at a climbable angle. Then they had to walk back through weeds and briars to get to their cars and trucks.

They never returned to the river. Their bathing was done each day in the little creek below the manse. Nor did they ever come back to Cow Creek. That was to be their first and their last visit.

Wilson and Eudella Gabbard were wonderful, working with our young people. Eudella taught the Young People's

Sunday School Class, and she and Wilson planned trips to Opryland, Myrtle Beach, King's Island and other places. Different projects were created to raise the necessary funds. The kids worked very hard in order to accumulate enough money for these trips. Those going to Myrtle Beach one summer were Freddie and Wilma Cooper, Pauletta and Henley McIntosh, Kenny and Lawanna Hensley, Garry and Greg Noble, Donna Gilbert and David Noble, Melissa Wilson, Selma Trosper, Juanita Smith, and Kathy Gabbard. Advisors were Wilson and Eudella Gabbard, Mossie McIntosh, Arvis Trosper, and Joe Powlas.

It was a wonderful trip. We camped in North Myrtle Beach, sleeping in tents, and doing our own cooking.

We went to Opryland, and a thunderstorm blew down all of our tents while we were gone for the day! That night, I slept in a tent filled with water and in a sleeping bag that was soaking wet. The next day my arms and legs ached with the flu, but never in my life had I had such an enjoyable and wonderful time.

Year after year we took the young people to Berea College for the outdoor drama "Wilderness Road," which they loved. They were also once taken to Pineville to see a performance of "The Book of Job." Though artistically well-done, it proved to be most dull and boring.

For several years, youth groups from the Lewinsville Presbyterian Church of McLean, Virginia, would come and spend the week with us; then, shortly afterwards, we would load up in the newly-given church van and head for Virginia to spend a week at their facility.

While visiting in Virginia we took time off to go to Washington, D.C. We toured the White House, the Smithsonian Institute, the Tomb of the Unknown Soldier, Mt. Vernon, and other points of interest. This trip was the highlight of the year for our youth activities!

I remember Benny Gabbard buying himself a new pair of shoes. Then he broke them in by walking on the sidewalks of Washington, D.C. all day and ended up with blisters on both feet.

Having just come from Cow Creek, it was a real chore driving in Washington, D.C. Jeanne Androit, in the lead car, remarked, "It's easy. Just follow me. You can't get lost!" She did not realize my frustration as I followed her car darting through the jammed traffic. I was terrified, fearful that one of the traffic lights would suddenly change, and we would be lost amid an abyss of lanes and lanes and lanes. Even today I have nightmares about driving a van loaded with kids, following an attractive redhaired lady rushing through traffic in downtown Washington, D.C.—going sixty miles per hour!

Every time I hear the song, "My Old Kentucky Home," I remember the parody written by the youth group from Westminster Presbyterian Church, from Akron, Ohio. They had dedicated it to the young people at Cow Creek. On their last night with us one summer, they gathered in the church and sang the following words to the tune of "My Old Kentucky Home:"

The sun shines bright in my Cow Creek White House
*   home,*
Where Toby[1] and Homer[2] do play!
And the pond runs dry, when the lard and molasses
*   fly,[3]*
And the fence is charged with 'lectric half the day.
Softball is the pastime,

---

[1]Toby—horse.
[2]First Homer—puppy.
[3]Initiation.

184

And Joe calls all the plays;
And he dances square, when the Akron kids are
   there,
And the plumbing keeps us running all the days.

When Arvis drives,
Tom and Howard let horseshoes fly;
While Homer[4] gets knocked on his can.[5]
Jimmy Ray eats frogs, while ole Herman slops the
   hogs,
And "Soupbean" catches flyballs on his head.

Bill and Dale catch grounders,
While Clint goes after girls.
And Ole Herbie smiles, while Bruce drives for many
   miles,[6]
So that Sue and Frances can see Charlie's curls.

Danny is the favorite,
And Phill shoots like a pro;
While Big Wallace grins,
As do Claude and Robert, too.
Donna cheers! and all come home to POPPA JOE.

Many letters were to be received following the departure of the youth groups. These were read then carefully tucked away. They all said the same thing: We love Cow Creek and we love the people and we want to come back again!

I remember well a youth group from one of the northern states. They had with them a rather staid, middle-aged lady who was their leader. When she snapped her fingers they moved—and they moved quickly. During her entire stay I never saw her smile one time. It seemed strange to me that

---

[4]Second Homer—boy.
[5]Shooting a 12-gauge shotgun.
[6]Driving church van for Sunday school, youth groups, etc.

such a woman would be chosen to be the advisor of a youth group. There were other adults with the group, but clearly, she was the one with the authority.

They arrived on a hot August day. After showing them the Summer White House, where they would be staying, they asked if they might go swimming.

"Of course," I replied. "We always go swimming about two o'clock down at the river, which is about four miles from here." The kids were all smiles. "Our young people will go with you."

Everyone hurried to his or her assigned quarters to change into bathing attire, but the lady in black, with her hair tied behind her head in a bun, remained. I could tell that she was deeply troubled. Finally, she asked, "Mr. Powlas,"—she paused for several seconds—"Mr. Powlas, do *your* young people wear . . . bathing suits?"

I thought that to be a strange question. Did she actually believe that we permitted our boys and girls to go swimming in the nude?

I answered, "No, they do not!"

She gasped, turned quickly, went into the kitchen and called a meeting of the other advisors. Within three minutes she returned and stated that, because of the unsanitary conditions of the river, their young people would not be swimming that week.

My laughter could be held no longer.

I quickly assured her that our young people did, indeed, wear bathing suits while swimming; that, in fact, some of our boys went swimming in their overall pants. I also assured her that the river was quite safe—and clean!

There was a shout of glee and a smattering of applause from the young people standing nearby; but the woman with the black horn-rimmed glasses and the knotted head of hair failed to appreciate my humor. Each day, rather than going swimming with the group, she remained at the Summer White House reading Shakespeare.

One week everything went wrong! Everything! A group from Dayton, Ohio, was visiting, and this was in the days before the Summer White House was opened, and everyone stayed in the manse.

They were a very nice group, most congenial, and I am sure that, being active within their church, they did not deserve what happened!

First, one of the girls drank diluted Clorox thinking that it was iced tea. We rushed her to the doctor, who immediately pumped her stomach. This gave us quite a scare.

Their intended project was to have been to build a tennis court at the church. We had a large parking lot which, actually, saw little use, so we all agreed that a tennis court would be a wonderful addition.

However, the wooden bridge leading up to the church was about ready to collapse. With constant high waters and floods each year, the sills had deteriorated terribly; so, the building of a new bridge certainly took priority over building a tennis court.

On Monday morning the young people began removing the top boards from the bridge floor, while the men of the church went into the hills to cut enough oak trees to build a new bridge. Jerry Wilson, at the sawmill, said that he would be glad to saw the timber for us, but he would need some help. Gene Moore volunteered to help.

Ed, the youth group's senior advisor, was with me as I went over to the sawmill to talk to Gene about the bridge, and I was standing there talking with Gene when he accidentally cut his hand on the large saw. Had I not been there it never would have happened, so I felt responsible for the accident!

187

Gene's cut began to bleed profusely. We put him into my car and immediately rushed him to the emergency room at the little Oneida Hospital where, incidentally, his wife, Lexene, had just delivered a baby the day before. Meantime, back at the sawmill, Ed had fainted at the sight of blood. The boys had picked him up, put him in the car and rushed back toward the manse, completely forgetting that the bridge was out! The brakes had been applied just in time. They turned the car around, drove down the road and through the creek back up to the manse. Ed was carried into the manse, still unconscious, and placed on the living room couch.

Gene got his hand patched up, Ed recovered, and the next day everything was back to normal. Local men from the creek gave us a hand and the sills were put in place, and the bridge was ready for the flooring.

It was suggested that since the constant splashing of high water had caused the deterioration of the sills, it would be a good idea to creosote all the wood before putting down the top flooring.

So we hurried down to Beattyville Lumber and Supply, purchased ten gallons of creosote and returned to the bridge where everyone was eager to begin.

Most of the young people who came to Cow Creek wanted to get a suntan while they were there. So, when the day began, everyone came to work in shorts. Having never used creosote before, we had failed to read the instructions which, in time, proved to be disastrous.

The young people straddled the logs with their buckets filled with creosote and their paint brushes and started applying the creosote. The sun was hot and they worked with zest. Every so often someone would take his or her camera and snap pictures as the work progressed. The entire area was permeated with a feeling of happiness and joy—with no realization of what was about to happen. They had worked all morning, and just before lunch, several of the adults went with me into Booneville for additional supplies.

Upon returning, I was met at the front door of the manse by Ed, who was frantic. Most of the young people were lying on the floor, holding their groin area, moaning, crying, and sobbing. It was a very pathetic sight and we could see that they were in great pain. It immediately became apparent what had caused their problem.

We rushed to Beattyville—16 miles away—to the doctor. At that time there was just one doctor serving two counties (Owsley and Lee) with a combined population of more than 10,000 people!

"Dr. Broadus," I said, "A lot of young people have been in contact with creosote over a period of several hours and they have been burned by it. Is there something that you can give me to ease their pain?"

"Yes, there is," he replied, and he and his nurse hurriedly filled a bag with jars of ointment. We rushed the sixteen miles back to Cow Creek.

The girls were put in one room and the boys in another. They could not wait to start applying the ointment. We discovered, however, we had only about half enough. Again, we got into the car and rushed back to Beattyville. This time the doctor gave me all the ointment he had on hand and sent me to a local drug store for an additional supply, which proved to be adequate. I had no idea that a human being could receive a burn from creosote. Since that incident, I *always* read the instructions when using something for the first time.

It was truly a week that will long be remembered. But it was not a *total* loss. Friday night all of the kids went over to Annville and roller-skated 'til midnight!

On Wednesdays we would always take the visiting youth

groups to the stock sale, which was held just outside of Booneville, about two miles up Lerose Road. They watched the auctioning of the mules, cows, and hogs and looked on with interest at the swapping of knives or the buying of pistols. It was a very colorful and happy event, the social event of the week. Our local people looked forward to seeing friends and relatives again. There would be as many as five or six hundred people there during the course of the day. Some people came to buy, some came to sell, and others just came to "look around."

One day while we were there with a group, a young boy came running up to me. "Joe, they've got a St. Bernard over there, and they only want twenty-five dollars for it."

They had all heard about my love for dogs—especially boxers and St. Bernards and at the time, I did not have a dog.

The young people quickly pooled their resources, looked toward me pleadingly, then led me over to a beautiful large friendly St. Bernard.

"I have his papers, he's pedigreed," the man said as he handed me the papers to examine. The papers looked authentic. The dog, known as Samuel Todd III, was registered and there were other names to verify ownership.

"Do you want him?" the kids asked in unison.

It seemed like a good deal to me. A pedigreed St. Bernard for only twenty-five dollars! "Let's get him!" was my reply.

I gave the man the twenty-five dollars the kids had collected. Proudly, they led the dog back to the van and quickly placed him in the seat. Exactly six weeks later Samuel Todd III gave birth to six beautiful little St. Bernard puppies! No one ever dreamed—or thought to look—that *he* was a *she!*

The most *unusual* group ever to come to Cow Creek was the Ecumenical Youth Group which arrived one summer and stayed for one week.

Two men from New York had arrived prior to the Ecumenical Group and the question was asked, "Since some of the Ecumenical Group will be black, will there be any adverse reaction from any of your people?"

My reply was simple and honest. "I really don't know. I don't foresee any problems. Cow Creek is known for its friendliness and for its hospitality."

It turned out to be a great week. Lisane Work Woubou, from Ethiopia, taught the Adult Sunday School class on Sunday morning. Emmanuel Nsuba Boo, of Leopoldville, in the Congo, talked with our farmers about agriculture; as did Samuel Nassif Mansour, who was from the Government Agricultural School in Shambaat, in the Sudan. They had lengthy conversations with Sam Thomas over on Indian Creek.

Rosemarie Lindmair, of Germany, had never eaten turnips or gravy. Sergio Roca, from Cuba; Bonnie Stobo, from New Jersey; Kar Yin Fung, from the Hong Kong Theological Seminary; Garry Gepfert and Melinda King, from Texas, and Reverend and Mrs. Sunny Pek-Ho Oey were among those who picked blackberries and milked cows for the first time. There was also mule riding; swimming in the Kentucky River; horseshoe tournaments; rifle and shotgun matches; softball games; helping in our Vacation Bible School, and worshipping together.

The last night the group was here more than two hundred persons gathered for our final service. Each guest spoke about his own country. Then, in closing, the lights were turned out and only a single candle was left burning. Beginning with Kar Yin Fung, from Hong Kong, and ending with Rosemarie Lindmair, from Germany, each delegate prayed the Lord's Prayer in his native language. Then, joining hands, in unison we all prayed the Lord's Prayer in English.

One delegate later wrote, "I know that you can never get

a complete picture of any country, and it is even more difficult to get one of such a huge country as the United States. There I saw that not all people in the States live the luxurious prosperous life as we see it in the movies. So, be sure that I'll never forget Kentucky!"

There is a sincere warmth and a beautiful simplicity about the people of Kentucky. Perhaps that is why the Caravan's itinerary included a week at Cow Creek.

As a creek, we all were thrilled and honored when Joyce Ann Moore, active in our youth work and a member of the YOUTH FOR CHRIST team, after winning the Southeastern Conference Championship, went on to Winona Lake, there winning the National Championship! Cow Creek was a part of a national championship!

We made movies for our youth work. Filmstrips were shown. There were the ball games, the picnics, the treks to the top of the mountains, the horseshoe games and the square dancing, but nothing was as important, nor more beautiful, than when one of those boys or girls knelt in the sanctuary of our church and received Christ as his or her personal Savior. It was then that one felt a joy that was to last through the years, which, in time, would comfort and sustain a tall, lanky preacher as he went his way, sharing as best he could the love of Christ.

13

In the ministry the most difficult of all duties is conducting the funeral. As one grows older, and as the minister becomes more entrenched within the community, this task becomes extremely hard. A funeral involves the entire valley and, when one person dies, everyone within the church dies just a little. In the mountain area there is a strong bond, a comradeship that is without equal: Our people walk together, work together, worship together, and sorrow together, and when death comes neither the community nor the church can ever be the same again. Death, inevitable and often unexpected, is the most difficult burden to accept, to understand, and to bear.

Strange that I am unable to remember my first funeral; and, since the little black book was lost years ago, I have no idea as to who, where, or when the event occurred. But there have been funerals that left an indelible mark upon my life.

He was a young boy, only sixteen years of age, and his name was Charles. Although he lived here on the creek, Charles never attended any of our youth meetings, nor do I ever remember his being in church. He and his family were always working, so a Sunday became the same as a Tuesday or Friday to him. Tall, strong, quiet and handsome, he was beloved and respected by everyone within our valley. There was also a twin sister, equally as remarkable as the boy; and, she, too, was beautiful, with the same wholesome qualities as her brother.

The family had an extremely difficult time, remaining constantly in debt. (On one occasion I had to go to Hyden to get the father out of jail where he had been charged with writing a bad check.) For Charles, there was never a day of rest, never a ball game with the young people here on the creek.

Whenever I had a conversation with Charles, he was either in the fields or sitting by the side of the road working on an old truck, trying to get it in running condition again; however, he would always be smiling. The machinery with which they baled hay rarely worked a full day without a breakdown, but through the use of wire, a screw, and a lot of hard labor, the day's chores were always accomplished. Charles and his family were the first on the creek to arise in the morning, and they were the last to go to bed at night.

Theirs was a happy life and we admired them for the great love and affection that was shared with each other— especially between father and son—and for the deep bond that was so evident within their family life. Laughter abounded in the fields. Occasionally one would hear the father singing in a deep bass voice. The women, being good cooks, filled the table with potatoes, shuck beans, corn-bread, ham and chicken.

Late at night, I could often hear the clank, clank of the old tractor and the hay baler as the father and son made their way home. No job was too menial, no task was too large; mostly, the day consisted of the baling of hay. They worked for people not only here on Cow Creek but also on Indian Creek, Meadow Creek, and around and beyond Booneville.

It was late evening, just about dusk, and Charles had hurriedly returned from Indian Creek where he had gone to get some spices for his mother, who was canning pickles. He turned into their driveway too quickly and, from the porch where she was waiting, his mother saw the tractor overturn, pinning her son beneath. In panic, she ran down the creek to the nearest neighbor, and, although an ambulance took Charles to the Irvin Hospital, he lived only a few hours. Young Charles was dead.

Word spread fast and, within a few minutes, everyone on Cow Creek and Indian Creek knew about the death of this young boy. Only a few hours before, he and his father had been out in the fields working, singing, and laughing. Now Charles was dead. It seemed so cruel, so sad to lose that boy; and, for a family who had so little, I am sure the loss seemed more than they could bear.

When the hour for the funeral arrived, the Cow Creek Presbyterian Church was completely filled. The choir sang two numbers, "The Old Rugged Cross," and "What a Friend We Have In Jesus." Then, with tears in my eyes, and praying that my voice would not break, I read the Twenty-third Psalm. They were country people, farmers, and I felt that the role of the shepherd would be comforting. I remember looking down at the mother. There was no crying, no tears. Only deep profound sorrow. A strong person, through the years she had learned to endure pain and sorrow. Her face was set, as in granite. Her eyes looked straight ahead, never moving from the inexpensive gray casket before her. Her worn and tired hands, folded, trembled every so often.

We buried Charles in the most beautiful plot in the new cemetery, just below the large white cross. Years later, the family moved to Ohio; but always, once a year, they return-ed on Memorial Day to place flowers on his grave, and they *always* placed a twenty dollar bill in my hand for the upkeep of the cemetery. It was difficult to accept the money, know-ing of their financial hardships, but not to do so would have offended them. So, I always took the money, and on the following Sunday it was placed in the offering in memory of a boy who worked all of his life, who never played ball, and who died doing an errand for his mother.

Through the years whenever there was a funeral with an abundance of flowers, I would take a basket and place it on Charles's grave. In some special way, the beauty of the flowers helped to take away the loneliness and the sadness of his grave.

Every minister remembers well his most embarrassing moment, that time when he literally wants to die, when he feels about two inches tall. My moment came during a funeral.

There was an elderly man in our church who constantly gave me trouble. Not any great amount, but just enough to make life miserable and to keep me from enjoying life to its fullest. I was tall—six feet four—weighed about one hundred and thirty pounds and had a horrible inferiority complex. I could excel in nothing—absolutely nothing. My only claim to success was in my preaching. Though I worked long and hard on my sermons, this man constantly found fault— nothing of any great importance, but just enough to remind me that I, being a young inexperienced minister, certainly could and should do better. (Later, after years of experience in the ministry, I was to learn that those who criticize are usually insecure themselves and the giving of advice makes them feel important.)

Out of respect for his age I simply smiled and remained silent. Finally, in desperation, one night I fell to my knees, sobbing unto the Lord, asking for help. I was certainly doing my best. The Lord must have heard and understood, for within the week the old man died. (In all honesty, I am quite sure that my prayer had nothing to do with his death; nevertheless, there was profound gratitude for his passing!)

My most embarrassing moment was brought about through a tape recorder. Prior to a funeral the people would enter the sanctuary, take their seat and there would be absolute silence until the funeral began. Something was needed to upgrade the funeral service; so, with clothing sale money in hand, a trip was made to Lexington to Barney Miller's where a reel-to-reel tape recorder was bought. Then, from a record of religious organ music, several beautiful hymns were recorded. Before a funeral, the tape recorder would be placed in the sanctuary, the recorded organ music would be played, thus giving our church the dignity and the sanctity of an up-to-date, modern Presbyterian church. I marvelled at my brilliance!

About the same time the discovery was made that the tape recorder could be used for other purposes as well. Whenever a popular song was played on the radio, one simply recorded that song on the tape recorder. The secular songs were kept on one end of the tape, the religious hymns on the other.

During my absence, either some child turned a few knobs or else, accidentally, the tape was advanced too far. The church was hushed in mournful grief. The casket was being brought down the aisle to the beautiful musical strains of "God Be with You Till We Meet Again." Beautiful. Perfect. Such dignity. Then, suddenly—out of nowhere—Herb Alpert and the Tijuana Brass started blaring out "Save the Last Dance for Me." It took only a few seconds for me to reach the tape recorder, but those few seconds seemed like an eternity. The Lord knows that the happening was an accident, but, I am sure, the man who had always criticized me would have declared that his "being put away" by the Tijuana Brass was intentional—another one of my constant shortcomings.

His name was Clyde Gabbard and, when he died, I was unable to conduct the funeral, but I wanted to have some part, even some small part in the service, so I asked Lucy if I might have the Committal Service at the grave. The hardest and most difficult task of my entire ministry at Cow Creek was standing by Clyde's grave and reading from the *Book of Common Worship:*

"Unto the mercy of Almighty God, we commend the soul of our brother departed and we commit his body to the ground, earth to earth, ashes to ashes, dust to dust, in the sure and certain hope of the resurrection to eternal life, through Jesus Christ our Lord."

Standing there above his casket, looking out across the valley, I saw a man with a gun across his shoulder walking through the open fields. I saw the old green Chevrolet truck, come back from Booneville on a Saturday afternoon, turn from the main road then cross the little wooden bridge that led to his home. I saw a man with a tobacco knife in his hand, working strenuously to get the day's work done, working far too hard, doing the work of two men.

When I came to Cow Creek, Clyde was working in Grayson, Kentucky, and we saw him only in passing. When the job ended he came back to continue farming. But he was cold and withdrawn. Although Lucy, his wife, and the children came to church regularly, Clyde never attended.

One day while visiting his home, for the first time I had an opportunity to talk with Clyde. After visiting for a few minutes with the women who had gathered in one room, I wandered into the back room where the men were playing Rook. Several men spoke their greetings, but Clyde remained silent, resentful that the new preacher was endangering their game. Rook, which is played with colored numbered cards, is a most enjoyable game and everyone on Cow Creek played it, both young and old, and especially in the winter months.

My presence dampened their spirits and there was the feeling that they wanted me to leave, but their desire to get rid of me only strengthened my determination to stay.

After about an hour, during which time I thoroughly enjoyed watching them play, out of politeness one of the men asked if I wanted to play. Quickly, I consented.

"We'll play for a quarter a game," Clyde spoke sternly.

They had not been playing for money during my presence, and I was startled that he should suggest playing for twenty-five cents a game when I entered the game. Maybe he wanted to embarrass me; or, perhaps, he thought that it would be a way of getting me to leave.

"A quarter a game?" I asked puzzled.

He never raised his head. "A quarter a game."

Every man present smiled. They knew that no preacher would ever play for money.

"I won't play for money, but I will make a bet with you." Everyone became interested—especially Clyde. "If you lose the game, you come to church next Sunday morning."

The statement caught the men by surprise. They really wanted to play Rook, and this position gave everyone a way out with honor. After all, they reasoned, how could a young man from North Carolina ever compete against the seasoned professional Rook players of Kentucky. It was an easy bet.

"Okay, sounds good to me," Clyde answered, knowing that there would be no contest.

But the young preacher from North Carolina was the one who had an ace in the hole. The summer before coming to Cow Creek, he had served the First Presbyterian Church of Sweetwater, Tennessee, and every Thursday night the professional men of the town gathered and played Rook. During Dr. Greenhoe's (the pastor of the church) vacation, he had

Cow Creek Presbyterian Church in Winter.

been asked to take his place, so, a young seminary student learned to play Rook from experienced and dedicated men. But, even more important, he loved to play Rook. So, unknown to the smiling men, he was ready and anxious for the challenge.

It was a long, difficult game and my partner, out of loyalty to Clyde, certainly did not help our cause. But I won, and in winning, Clyde lost. No camera, no artist could possibly have captured the expression on Clyde's face when he realized that he had been defeated, that he had lost the game to an outsider—and a preacher at that. It was an expression of anger, disbelief, and disgust.

Although extremely upset at the defeat, Clyde Gabbard was an honest man, and when Sunday came, he was in church. Through the years that followed, no person other than Rudolph Turner ever attended church more faithfully. There was a certain row, a certain place, where Clyde always sat. Though he would never agree to be an Elder or teach a Sunday school class, he always came to church on Sunday mornings. Faithfulness is one of the greatest virtues of the Christian faith, and through rain, sleet, and snow, Clyde Gabbard came to church.

At first there was a coldness, a distance that seemed almost insurmountable, but in time, Clyde became more friendly, and I learned to accept his quietness and aloofness. Our friendship developed slowly, but gradually.

His brother, Ed, was in the television business, so Clyde and Lucy had a television installed. This meant putting an antenna, a booster, and a converter at the top of the mountain, then running the track wire several thousand feet to the house below. As a rule this cost more than the television set itself. Since I had no television I would go out to Clyde's in the morning and watch the seven o'clock news on the NBC "Today Show." The news had always been important to me.

It was essential to my personal life and to my ministry, so rarely did I miss a morning.

For fifteen years this became my regular schedule. Monday through Friday I would go out to Clyde and Lucy's. While she prepared breakfast, I would go with Clyde when he went to milk the cows. After breakfast (I never ate, but I would drink a cup of coffee) we would watch a portion of the "Today Show."

Once, while in New York, I went down to 49th Street early one morning to the window studio where the program originated at that time, held up a sign "HELL-O COW CREEK, KENTUCKY," but Clyde and Lucy, unaware of the plan, missed my brief appearance on national television.

Only on one occasion had I ever fired a gun prior to coming to Kentucky. One of the local boys had brought a single shot rifle up to the dormitory at the Crossnore School down in North Carolina, and although it had been against the rules, we went over to the other side of Christmas Tree Hill and had a shooting match. I was fascinated. Men in North Carolina had guns, and also dogs that they took along with them when they went bear hunting. That one brief moment had instilled within me the desire to own a gun.

Sam Cornett, a school teacher on Cow Creek, learned of my eagerness to secure a gun, and through his generosity I was able to purchase an excellent, almost new, .22 automatic rifle. The gun was actually a gift, worth far more than the ten dollars I had given.

Clyde loved to shoot; so, when he learned that I had a rifle, he came out to the manse just about every day and we would have a shooting match. An excellent marksman, he carefully and methodically taught me the proper use and care of the gun.

A target was needed, so we selected the electric light pole

202

in the backyard of the manse. It was an ideal target: just the right distance and, even more important, we could sit on the back step of the manse and shoot.

In time, we had shot the pole almost in two, and it was left hanging by the electric wires. A call was made to Jackson RECC in McKee, informing them of our need for a new pole. They quickly assured me that the pole we already had was a new pole and there was no way that it was about to fall. When they learned that their pole had been shot in half by someone shooting target practice, they were furious. The pole was replaced without charge, but the admonition was clear that the next pole would be replaced at cost.

So, Kentucky opened unto Joe Powlas a new world; a world of Rook, family church suppers and youth groups, C.E., swimming in the river and, for awhile, I reveled in shooting. In fact, all of my spare money went for shells.

Clyde and I bought sticks of dynamite (which were, at the time, legal to purchase), and these were placed on top of the old camp kitchen, down the hill from the church. By using hollow-point shells, the dynamite, when hit, produced a tremendously loud explosion. The cows and horses were frightened, and there were several complaints that "there was too much noise down around the church," so we discontinued shooting at the sticks of dynamite, but it was great fun while it lasted.

One morning as we walked up to the barn to do the milking, Clyde smiled and asked, "Have you ever killed a squirrel?"

"No," I replied.

"Today," he spoke quietly, "I promise you that you will get your first squirrel."

We watched Frank Blair give the news on the "Today" program and, after two cups of coffee, Clyde got up. He

went into the bedroom and brought back two guns, his priz-
ed Nitro Hunter and a Remington automatic.

He handed me the Remington. Then we went down to
Oak Wilson's and walked up the hollow about a mile. "Why
are we going here?" I asked. He motioned for me to be quiet.
We continued to walk. Every so often I would ask a question
and he, in turn, without speaking would motion for me to be
absolutely quiet.

Finally, we stopped and he pointed straight ahead.
"There," he whispered. "There in the mulberry tree." "Which
is the mulberry tree?" I asked, puzzled.

"There." Again he pointed straight ahead. "There in the
mulberry tree." I could tell he was irritated.

"Clyde," I hesitated, "I don't know a mulberry tree from
a sycamore tree."

"Damn it! Shoot it!" he cried angrily.

Something moved and I squeezed the trigger. The .12
gauge shotgun gave forth a deafening roar, and I saw a
brown object fall to the ground. I knew both joy and sorrow
in that moment. Joy because I had become a hunter, but sorrow in realizing that I had taken the life of an animal.

Rook became the great event of the week. We played on
Saturday nights in different homes: Gene Moore's, Rudolph
Turner's, Shelby Moore's, Peter McIntosh's, Clyde
Gabbard's, Carl Steppe's, or at the manse. I prepared my sermons during the week so that my Saturday nights would be
free. (Should a death or serious illness occur within our community, we would not play.)

One Saturday night the Rook game had been held at Carl
Stepp's. Carl was a good player, putting heart and soul into
his game—the kind of person one really likes to play against.
It makes the game far more interesting, and what joy to win
over an opponent who doesn't like to lose!

That night Carl and Norman had won every game. Clyde and I, playing as partners, had lost every game.

Returning home about eleven o'clock, at the mouth of Cow Creek, Clyde said, "Joe, stop the car."

"What's wrong?" I asked.

"Stop the car!"

As soon as the car had stopped Clyde got out, walked over to the bridge and quickly threw my new deck of Rook cards into the river. Then, getting back into the car, he calmly said, "That's the last time we will ever play with that deck." I bemoaned losing the games that night, but more, I bemoaned the two dollars that I had paid for the deck.

Year after year I went with Clyde to take his tobacco to Lexington; and, year after year we would stand in the coldness of the large warehouses waiting for the sales. A few dollars per hundred pounds meant the difference between trading trucks or buying a new shotgun. If the year had been a good one, and the price had been right, we would stop by a certain pawnshop in downtown Lexington. There, Clyde would trade guns.

One year, while he was looking at a gun, I discovered a Leica camera for only twenty-five dollars. Borrowing ten dollars from Clyde, I was able to purchase my first good camera. Though old, it was in perfect condition; but, most important, it was a *Leica*.

Clyde had the strange habit of naming an article he had purchased after the previous owner's wife. When he bought Roy Reynold's Chevrolet truck he promptly named the truck Eva. Quite often we heard, "Eva just wouldn't start this morning," or "I need to take Eva down and get the oil changed."

He bought a cow from Lucian Burch and, again, the cow became known as Georgia Lou, the name of Lucian's wife.

Georgia Lou, in time, became quite a roaming cow and simply would not stay put. She loved to explore, jumping fences and going to greener pastures. One morning, ready to go to Lexington for hospital calls, I noticed Lucy and the girls chasing Georgia Lou. (Clyde had gone to work.) There is no joy or excitement in chasing a cow while wearing one's good shoes and one's Sunday suit; but they needed help so, quickly, I ran after the errant beast. We chased Georgia Lou from one field to another, across the creek, up the hollows, trying desperately to head her back toward the barn. She absolutely refused to go. Finally, finding a short piece of a two-by-four, I hit Georgia Lou on the rump with every ounce of strength within me. She turned around immediately and humbly walked to the barn. I went on to Lexington for hospital calls.

Someway, somehow the word spread about my chasing the cow. In Booneville several days later, the question was asked, "Preacher, how in the world could you possibly hit such a sweet old *lady?*" I smiled weakly, then walked away. No need in trying to explain that I had actually hit the *cow*—not the *lady.* The joke had gone too far for that.

A letter came asking if I would go to 475 Riverside Drive, New York, to speak during a morning service at the Mecca of the Presbyterian Church U.S.A. My car was in the garage in Beattyville; so, about four a.m. one morning, I rode with Clyde to Lexington to catch a plane to New York. Clyde was taking a load of tobacco to Lexington to market. Several days later he picked me up, which, incidentally, happened to be the same day that his tobacco sold.

I clearly remember the last Sunday that Clyde Gabbard came to church. Mary Belknap Gray—whose grandfather had founded Belknap Hardware in Louisville—came to visit with us at Cow Creek. I had come to know her through the

Kentucky Bookmobile Program. She originally planned to stay only two days, but ended up staying two weeks. She was an elderly lady who always traveled with her companion, Marjorie Smith.

That Sunday morning in my prayer I had made the remark that there was one person present who may not return again, and of course, I was referring to Mary Gray who was more than ninety years of age. Little did I know that it was to be the last service for Clyde, or that Mary Gray was to return several more times.

On that same Sunday afternoon I drove Mary Gray and Marjorie Smith back to Louisville. Since the journey had been more than two hundred miles, they had made arrangements for me to spend the night.

The following Monday morning I was not at Cow Creek to go with Clyde to do the milking; and, that day, while working for the Highway Department, Clyde had a heart attack.

The heart attack occurred in August, and for weeks it was not known if Clyde would survive or not. We came to know every picture, every magazine in the waiting room of the Lexington Central Baptist Hospital. Hour after hour we waited and, hour after hour, we prayed for his recovery.

As a church, we prayed and as a community, we prayed. In time, he came back home but there was a difference. He was not the same Clyde Gabbard that we had known through the years. The body was there, but the life had gone.

One Saturday morning in March, a car raced up the hill to the manse. I met Verne at the door and she cried, "Joe, come quickly. It's Daddy."

His hour had finally come. For a moment I could not move. My feet seemed nailed to the floor and there was difficulty in breathing, but quickly, we got into the car and I drove out to the house where a crowd had gathered. There was a strange hushed silence as they motioned me into the far room. I walked into the bedroom where his body was lying on the floor. He looked so thin, so frail, so totally different from the man who had once hunted and worked the fields. His eyes were closed and there was no breathing. Slowly I fell to my knees and tenderly placed my hand on his shoulder.

"Clyde?"

Someone put an arm around me, helping me to my feet, then blindly I stumbled out of the house and into the yard. As in a dream, I then walked back up to the barn where every morning for fifteen years, we had gone to milk together; and finding the three-legged stool on which Clyde had sat as he milked, I sat down, placed my head into my hands and cried for a long, long time.

14

A minister is often called on to conduct a funeral for a person he does not know, or in a church to which he has never even been.

I was once asked to perform just such a service. The man was from Ohio, and the funeral was to be held in a small church on the other side of the county. Directions were carefully given on how to reach the church, and I had no trouble finding the small white building, seldom used. Following a service the minister always precedes the casket; so, humbly, I took my place in the procession to suddenly realize that, since I had never been to this church before, I did not know where the cemetery was located. As we walked slowly down the outside steps of the church, I quickly asked a man standing just a few feet away where the cemetery was. His reply was to follow the little path to the right; so, obediently, we followed the path as directed. (I presumed the pallbearers were just as unfamiliar as I was to the area.) With the casket and the few mourners following, I led the procession through the woods right up to the front door of the outdoor toilet. There the path ended.

After turning around and retracing our steps, we found the right path and went to the cemetery at the top of the hill where the man from Ohio was respectfully buried. There had been *two* paths, and I had followed the one used most often.

How can I ever forget the agony of one man's funeral. His widow insisted on every detail being perfect. He was a prominent citizen and hundreds would be attending his funeral; so everything had to be correct and proper and right. No stone was left unturned to assure that his funeral would be remembered for a long, long time.

After three long, hard arduous days the funeral came to pass. Indeed, everything was done in the best of taste. The choir sang only the most complicated anthems; my black robe was used for the occasion, and the county sheriff's car—with blue lights flashing—led the funeral procession to the cemetery. (The blue light is never used when some poor *insignificant* soul passes away.)

Several days later, I conducted another funeral at the funeral home. There were few in attendance, no choir to sing, no flashing blue light to lead the procession; but after the service, an old man in clean, faded blue overalls came up to me and placed a ten dollar bill in my hand. I returned the money, explaining that I wanted to do the service without pay, out of respect for the deceased. He smiled and tears filled his eyes. He took both of my hands in his, held them for a few moments, thanked me, then turned and walked to an old beat-up truck.

The widow of the prominent citizen had never thanked me, never gave a penny to the church for the services, and never so much as wrote a note of appreciation; but the old man in the faded blue overalls wanted to give me ten dollars. I am sure that the ten dollars was as important to him as was a thousand dollars to most other people.

One of my most unusual funerals happened when I first

entered the ministry, back in the days when many corpses were not embalmed.

There was one elderly woman who lived to be one hundred years of age, and many thought that she would last another ten years. Right up until her final hours, she cooked, cleaned house and washed clothes. A joyful person, people loved to visit with her, for she was well-known and beloved throughout the territory.

Prior to her death she had requested not to be buried on Cow Creek. She wished to be returned to Indian Creek, where she and her husband had spent most of their married lives; so, after the service in the Cow Creek Church, the homemade casket was placed in a truck which we all followed. When we reached the foot of the hill on Indian Creek, we who had cars had to get out and walk up the little, steep, narrow road leading to the cemetery. The truck with the casket, after many jars and jolts, finally came to a halt at the top of the hill.

Prior to the committal service several of the women wanted to take "one last look" at the dear departed soul; so, reluctantly, the funeral director opened the wooden casket. The women jumped back in fear—with shock and disbelief etched on their faces. Inside the casket rested the one hundred-year-old woman with her eyes wide open. Her mouth was also open. That night I never slept a wink, nor was sleep to come for several nights following her burial.

During my entire ministry I only saw one person actually die. His name was Abe McIntosh.

One cold winter night there was a knock on the front door of the manse. When I opened the door two of the McIntosh boys were standing there. "Joe, would you please drive us to Oneida Hospital to see Dad? They say he won't last long."

"I'll try," I said softly. "It's awfully bad out there with all that snow, and the roads are icy. The temperature is six below zero, so I am not sure my car will start, but I'll certainly give it a try."

Fortunately, my car started. We headed out—on icy roads and a temperature that hovered around six below zero—and drove very cautiously, going not more than fifteen miles per hour. We arrived in time at the little mountain hospital, about thirty miles away.

The old man was sleeping. The two sons spoke to their father, somehow hoping that their words would be heard and understood. I knelt by the side of the bed, placed his hand in mine, and offered a prayer. As I prayed, his breathing became more peaceful. We all remained at his bedside until he died about an hour later.

The day of the funeral was the coldest ever recorded for that day in Kentucky, with the temperature dropping to twenty-two below zero. This time my car would not start. So, with several other people from the creek, we walked up the road and on up the hollow, placing scarves around our faces to protect us from the bitter cold. The trees cracked as we walked through the hills.

The funeral was conducted inside the home. I took my place by an open fireplace and, with Bible in hand, spoke of Nimrod, who was a mighty hunter. The women sat in homemade chairs. The children sat quietly on the floor. The men all stood, and those who were unable to get inside simply leaned by the door, trying to keep warm as best they could.

Following the simple service, the old man's homemade casket was placed on a sled, and a mule pulled the sled about a mile up the mountain behind the home. I was surprised at the large number of people who battled the subzero temperature to walk to the cemetery at the top of the mountain; but they had loved him, and this was the last time they could be in his presence. So, without speaking, we all walked, but we encountered difficulty walking in the frozen snow, and following the committal service there was difficulty in getting the frozen dirt back into the grave.

Years later, while walking with Clyde as he hunted, we came upon the little cemetery and he pointed out Abe's grave. It was a beautiful place; far removed from the clamor and the confusion of the world; peaceful and quiet and one truly felt, while standing there, the presence and the beauty of God.

His name was Estill McIntosh, but everyone called him Roy Rogers. He was buried on the hill behind his house, here on Cow Creek. His was a strange life, and there was something unique about Roy that continually haunted a person. His father was in the penitentiary. His mother had married an older man by the name of Charlie Red. Charlie Red was a graduate of Berea College and, at one time, had been one of the outstanding men of our county. But I knew Charlie Red only as an old man, a man who sold shaving cream, shaving blades, toilet articles, and soap.

The family lived in a house across the creek and there was no bridge nor foot-log near the house. The children walked a quarter-of-a-mile down the creek to a foot-log, but not Charlie Red. He waded the creek barefooted even in the coldest of weather. His secret was to drink a cup of boiling coffee just before entering the water, and then, once home again, to drink another cup of boiling coffee. The coffee pot stayed on the stove continuously.

Knowing that he had been married several times, one day I asked, "Charlie, how many children do you have?"

With a twinkle in his eye and poking me in the ribs, he replied, "Twenty-one—that I know of!" He was a man of much laughter and, evidentially, he was also a man of much life.

Roy Rogers was his stepson. Why the nickname "Roy Rogers," I never knew.

Roy's funeral was the largest attended funeral ever conducted in the Cow Creek Presbyterian Church. Chairs had been set up even in the backroom and, these, too, were filled. Not an empty seat remained.

During my early ministry, on Sunday morning, I would take my car, go up and down the creek, picking up those who had no transportation. (Years later, the Presbyterian Church in McLean, Virginia, would present to the Cow Creek Church a Ford Van that the young people had secured through collecting TV stamps.) Then, after my run, the Adult Sunday Class would be taught. This I thoroughly enjoyed. Sitting on the back of my seat, I faced the men and the women. We had many wonderful discussions as we studied the Bible together. Following the Sunday School Class, there was, of course, the sermon at the eleven o'clock service.

Roy Rogers came to church faithfully. An authority on wildlife, he knew the habitats of all the wild animals on Cow Creek, and he spoke with much intelligence in the native brogue of the creek. I was amazed at how much he knew concerning the common squirrel and the honey bee. (Years later, he was to teach soldiers in the hills of Korea.)

When I first came to Cow Creek—only twenty-three years of age—I dreaded the coming of nightfall. My early life had been spent at Crossnore, a D.A.R. School for Mountain Children in western North Carolina, and there had been two hundred children there. Following my stay at Crossnore, I attended Catawba College, in Salisbury, North Carolina, and there were over eight hundred people enrolled there. In Louisville Seminary there had been about two hundred persons.

Baptizing by immersion in the Kentucky River.

Then I came to Cow Creek and lived alone in a large, rambling, two-story manse (which had once been a dormitory) that was close to the Callahan cemetery. When evening approached, there was always dread and fear. I had nightmares about people breaking into the manse; nightmares about people coming out of their graves; and nightmares about voices that could be heard coming out of bodies that could not be seen.

An invitation had come asking me to speak at the College Hill Presbyterian Church, in Cincinnati, Ohio. Although arrangements had already been made for my overnight stay, I decided to return to my beloved Cow Creek; so, after a five-hour drive, I arrived back on the creek about two a.m. As I drove up the hill to the manse, once again I began experiencing a gnawing fear—dreadful fear of the dark, and fear of entering the huge old building. Then, too, it had been raining, consequently giving the darkened manse an even more ghostlike appearance.

With shaking hands and my breath coming in quick gulps, I slowly opened the front door. How I dreaded entering that dark building! Turning the living room lights on, I saw two feet protruding from the end of the living room couch. Two huge feet. I was unable to speak. I could not move. Two feet and a body were on the living room couch.

"It's me," Rogers said calmly raising up. "Hope you don't mind. I was out hunting and it started to rain. The front door was unlocked. I figured, you being a preacher, you wouldn't mind."

I was still unable to speak.

"If you don't mind, I'll just stay the rest of the night."

In numbness a pillow was secured, then a quilt. Weakly, I climbed the stairs to my bedroom. Never had I ever been so frightened before—never!

He scared me again not too much later. The Presbyterian Church of Owsley County was having a revival in Booneville, and each night I drove the large old bus, carrying people from Cow Creek and Indian Creek to the revival.

Since the bus could only carry about fifty people, we alternated nights, first carrying the people from Cow Creek, then the people from Indian Creek. The bus was always filled.

I remember one night espeically well. It had been a good service, with a powerful sermon being preached by the visiting Evangelist. I had played the piano, and everyone sang the old gospel hymns with spirited voices. Suddenly, alone on the bus (I had just finished unloading the last passenger over on Indian Creek and I was heading back for Cow Creek), I, too, started to sing. The engine was making a rather loud noise, so I sang that much louder! In fact, I sang as loud as I could.

It must have been around eleven o'clock for all of the houses were dark. Probably two reasons for my singing were the darkness and the fact that I was alone—alone on a lonely road, completely surrounded in darkness, so I sang as loudly as possible.

Suddenly, a hand was placed on my shoulder and a voice pierced the darkness. "What in the hell are you so happy about?"

I panicked! I turned loose the steering wheel. Immediately the bus left the road and went for a long way along the ditch line, but, miraculously, I grabbed the wheel and got it straightened out before the bus turned over.

My hands were shaking. My voice even more so. "Rogers! What are you doing here? This is Indian Creek's night. You live on Cow Creek."

"Now, preacher, don't get riled. I know it's Indian Creek's night. But I walked to town, went to the revival, and

I guess I just dreaded that long walk back home. So, when you weren't looking, I got on the bus and stayed real quiet back in the back." Although it was dark, I knew he was smiling. "You don't mind, do you?"

They brought his body back from Korea and the service was held in the Cow Creek Presbyterian Church with full military honors. Soldiers came from Fort Knox; there were two of his buddies who came from Korea, and in the congregation that day there were many officers of high rank.

Mary Kennedy Stamper walked with me up to the cemetery nestled high on the hill. Once again, as Charlie Red had done so many years before, when we came to the creek we took off our shoes and waded the water.

It was a beautiful summer day, quiet and peaceful. When the bugler played "Taps" one could feel, as never before, the eternal presence and the love of a mighty God. Looking out across the valley one could see the woods and the fields where he once trapped and hunted, a place he loved so deeply; and, with heads bowed, we all knew that, once again, the hunter was home.

I had a dream last night. For a little while I stood by her grave; and then, by some mysterious power, there was the searching for a rainbow; a rainbow that, for a brief moment, could be seen but, then, suddenly would disappear.

Then, strangely, I walked up and down the valley seeking desperately to find a bird with a broken wing. My dream took me to her home, but the lamp in the window was no longer lit, and weeds had grown up around the stone house. Where once there had been roses, I now found thorns and briars. There was no laughter as we once had known it years ago.

Ever so often, while in a crowd I see her face, but, when approached, the person always is a stranger. Her voice rings out so clearly on a Sunday morning from the choir, even though I know so well that she is not there.

When word comes that there is a need within the community—a concern for an elderly person—I immediately remember her kindness and compassion for the poor, the old, the forgotten.

How well I remember her words, "Joe, they need clothing. Will you go down and visit with them? Maybe they would come to church if *you* would ask them. I have asked but they've given me the impression that they feel that they wouldn't fit in."

For a long time there had been a pain within her chest. Then, we learned that she had cancer. She always remained her same indomitable self, full of courage and strength. Even in the advanced stages she rode the riding mower, mowing the lawn, stating, "The pain is there whether I am still or whether I am active. I want to be doing something." Always there was that joy, that cheerfulness, that smile. Surely she was a person of great strength who strengthened, equally, those around her.

Only once did I ever see her differently. In the hospital, in Lexington, knowing that death was inevitable, after I had had prayer and started to leave, she reached out her hand and motioned for me to sit down. "Joe," though weak, her voice was steady. "Please stay a little longer. I have to talk with you. You are like a brother to me, and there are some things that you *must* know." She paused for a few minutes, then continued. "I know that I am going to die. I don't know exactly when, but I know now that it won't be long. Please don't say anything. Just sit and listen and let me talk."

There was pain, great pain, throughout her body. She spoke with difficulty, but with determination. Every so often she would stop for a few minutes, then continue. So I listened, for a long, long time. I listened as a minister; I listened as a brother; I listened as a person who had known the family for many years, and I listened as a friend. Finally, after talking for more than an hour, she closed her eyes and drifted off into a deep sleep. Her words troubled me. Tears filled my eyes, but I was grateful for her confidence, grateful that at that hour, as a minister, I could be present. Her words, confidential, left an indelible mark upon my life. They will remain a part of me as long as I live, giving me the strength and courage to face a troubled world.

Sometime later, remembering her conversation, I sat down and made a cassette tape and sent it to her, so it could be played, time and time again. My prayer was that it might bring comfort and consolation.

We had talked on different occasions about her funeral arrangements. But, one day, the telephone rang and the voice on the line was almost too weak for me to understand. "Joe," she whispered, "for my funeral it will be too hard on the choir to sing, so I don't want any singing. And even though I know it will be hard on you, I want you to conduct my funeral. All I want you to do is read the twenty-third Psalm and then," she paused. "I want you to play the tape that you made for me a while back."

Beautiful flowers surrounded her casket. The room was filled to capacity. Slowly, and with great difficulty, I read the twenty-third Psalm as she had requested, then I sat down. With head bowed, hands folded, and tears welling to my eyes, the tape recorder was turned on. I heard my voice filling the room as it was being played over the public address system.

"Lois, I would just like to sit and chat with you for a few minutes, and I guess what I am really trying to do is to say thank you. Thank you for just being Lois Reynolds.

"There was a beautiful song I heard often as a child growing up. We don't hear it now, but it went something like this:

" 'When you come to the end of a perfect day
And you sit alone with your thoughts;
And your heart rings out with a carol gay
For the joy that the day has brought.
Do you know what the end of a perfect day
Can mean to a tired heart?
When the sun goes down with a flaming ray
And dear friends have to part.

" 'Well, this is the end of a perfect day
Near the end of a journey, too.
And it leaves a thought that is big and strong
With a wish that is kind and true;
For memory has painted a perfect day
With colors that never fade,
And we find at the end of a perfect day
The soul of a friend we've made.'

"As I sit here, looking back across the years, I can say with all honesty that this has been a good life. We are grateful that you have been a part of our church. You know, years ago we had a women's group that was quite active—and you were a part of that group. Remember how we used to meet, Monday after Monday after Monday? Remember how the church van would pick the women up and they would quilt, usually in the manse and then, on occasion, in the different homes? The women got together and chatted, they had their fellowship, they had their enjoyment, and it was a great event in the life of our church.

"I remember it quite well: Lucy Eversole, Belle and Mary Eversole, Charity Smith, Mollie Baker, Lissie,

221

Eva, Lexene, Edna Eversole, Rosa Callahan, Belle McIntosh, Ethel and Boots, and, of course, Lois Reynolds.

"We are grateful for those days. Grateful for the many wonderful hours that the women spent together quilting and laboring for the Lord. Then, through the years, you were a part of our clothing sales. You, Lucy and Verna. You worked with the clothes, hour after hour, day after day, and it was hard work. Even when you had pain in your chest you continued to work. Through your labors, through your love and dedication, the clothing was sold and the money was used in the work of the church. So, Lois, again we are grateful for those years.

"The Cow Creek Church choir has the reputation of being an excellent choir, and through the years we have had a fellowship that has been unique. We loved to sing. You know Carl and Martha Stepp, they were blessed with a wonderful family of singers. They sang, you sang, and you were a part of our choir. 'Each Step I Take,' 'Whispering Hope'—we have all of this on tape and I am so glad we recorded the services. You were very much a part of our choir. Blessed with a beautiful voice, you sang in our church and you sang to the glory of the Lord. Truly, we are grateful.

"You know, I would like to tell you this now. I have been here thirty-two years, and in all of those years I have never heard one word about Lois Reynolds that was not good. That is quite a remark. You can't say that about many people. People admire you, they respect you, and they love you. And the reason is that you are a good person and you have been a wonderful blessing in this community and in our church. Lois, you are very much beloved. The words spoken about you have been words of praise and words of admiration.

"The one thing we recall most about your life is your radiance and joy. I am sure that you have had days where the rain has fallen quite heavily. I am equally sure that there have been days with storms, days when the heavy clouds in your life just would not go away; but, always, we remember the composure of your joy and of your happiness. In your going and in your coming, you gave forth a happiness and people caught that spirit and it became a part of their life as well.

"It pains us to know that you have pain, and many tears have been shed because of the cancer. Prayers have been offered on your behalf; still we pray that the will of God be done, not our will. You recall, in the Garden of Gethsemane, Christ prayed for the cup to be removed, but then, he prayed, 'Not my will but Thy will be done.'

"We do not understand why this has happened to you. In all of our knowledge and in all of our wisdom there is no answer; so, we simply put our faith and our trust in the Lord and say, 'Thy will be done.' Now we truly see through a glass darkly, but we believe, as Christians, that all things do work together for good to them that love the Lord.

"There are things far worse than death, and there are things far more painful than dying. Triumphantly, as Christians, we put our hand in the Lord's, going forth one day at a time. And so, Lois, though we cannot understand, we simply accept this illness by faith and, tearfully say, 'Thank you for being Lois Reynolds.'

(She had been so active within our community, within

223

our church. Always that strength, always that smile. In her early fifties, she was too young to die.)

"We know that death is inevitable. It happens to all of us. You may be a day, a month, or a year ahead of the rest of us here on the creek, but, in time, one by one, we, too, will take our place and leave just as those before us have done.

"There is a story in the Bible that speaks so well of the death of a Christian. You remember the story of the rich man and Lazarus. The Bible states that Lazarus, when he died, was carried by the angels to Abraham's bosom. I believe that, when the time comes for us to depart from this life, the most wonderful, the most joyous experience known to man happens when one beloved by the Lord is carried by the angels into the glory and into the beauty of heaven.

"When you pass away—it may be tomorrow, or it may be next year—but when you leave, a part of us will go with you.

"I simply wanted to say how much we have enjoyed being with you, and how much we all love you. You have been without a doubt the epitome of *noblesse oblige.*

"In time, we will join you . . . where there will be no tears, no more pain, only peace and love, and where man will live forever in the presence and in the glory of God.

" *'Because I live, ye shall live also.'* This is the hope of every Christian. *'Lo, I am with thee, even unto the end.'* This is the assurance of every Christian.

"Thank you, Lois, thank you. Thank you for being Lois Reynolds."

In my dream last night, once again I heard the singing of

the choir with all the old members: Roy and Eva Reynolds, Lois Reynolds, Kendall Robinson, Verne Callahan, Mike Gabbard, Clarence Gibson, Rudolph Turner, Lexene and Sharon, and they all sang beautifully of the Lord. For a little while, through a dream, we were all back at the church. Everyone was laughing, and there was happiness, and then, quite suddenly . . . I awakened!

John lived next door with Clyde and Lucy and I deeply loved the old man. It was said that not once in his lifetime had he ever spoken one word against another person. Kind and gentle, he walked slowly, always smiling.

Since Clyde was working, I often took John to the doctor. One day, as we were ready to go, he walked out to the car. Belle said, "John, go back and get your new hat. You should wear your new hat to the doctor."

"Nope," was his reply. "I am going to wear the hat that Joe gave me." With these words, he proudly placed upon his head a old beat-up hat that I had found in a box and had given to him.

Slowly the strength left John. We brought him back home from the hospital, knowing that nothing could be done.

I was not present when John died, but a strange and remarkable thing happened. Just before dying, he asked that he be helped out of bed and allowed to stand on the floor. After standing alone for a few minutes, he lay back down and died. It was said that his father had made the same request just before he, too, had passed away.

She was a beautiful person—shy, quiet and reserved. Her duties within our church consisted of arranging the flowers for the sanctuary and for our church suppers. For hours, Mary Eversole worked with wild flowers, twigs and leaves,

*Mary Kennedy Stamper and the author returning from
cemetery where Roy Rogers had just been buried.*

and her arrangements were artistic, beautiful, and most memorable.

Each Sunday she would walk out of the hollow, catch the church van, and come to our little church on Cow Creek. During her early life she had worked, arranging flowers in a sanatarium in Battle Creek, Michigan; but, in the early '50s, she returned to Cow Creek to live with her brother, Ed, and her older sister, Belle. None of the three ever married and they lived about two miles up the hollow from the main road.

Quite often, Mary would go to Lexington with me for shopping or to keep an eye appointment on Upper Street. While I made my hospital calls and collected needed items for the churches, she would do her shopping in downtown Lexington. Our meeting place would be at Sears, on Main Street.

If weather permitted when we returned, I would take her up the hollow; but, if the roads were wet, or if there was snow, she would walk from Lucy Eversole's, carrying her flashlight, then call me, when arriving home. This had been a routine we had practiced for years and years.

In time, Ed passed away and the two sisters lived alone. Junior Eversole, Gus Turner and I saw to their needs—getting their groceries, their coal and their wood. The house they lived in was an old house, but to them it was home; and they were content with the beautiful flowers in their garden, the outside well, the animals and birds which roamed freely in their yard.

Because of increasingly ill health, the sisters moved to Battle Creek, Michigan, to be with their two nieces. For several years they lived in a little home which was warm and comfortable, where they were well cared for.

Mary and Belle Eversole were deeply devoted to one another. When Mary was shopping in Lexington she was always concerned about Belle, insisting that we hurry back before dark lest Belle might become frightened.

Not only did they spend most of their entire lives together, it was said that both had remarked that, if one died, the other wanted to die at the same time. That was their one remaining desire, to die together.

Belle died at the age of ninety-seven in a nursing home. Mary, not knowing of Belle's sickness, nor of her death, passed away the following day at the age of ninety-five in a hospital about fifteen miles away.

A funeral service was held for the two sisters in Battle Creek; then, both caskets were brought back to Cow Creek together. After a graveside service the two sisters were placed in the ground, side by side, in the cemetery behind the Cow Creek Presbyterian Church.

All of the hospitals in Lexington were excellent and praiseworthy, each excelling in a special and a different way; but, to me, there was always a sadness about the University of Kentucky Medical Center, probably because this was where most of the poor people were admitted. As I made my rounds, sometimes several times weekly, there was always a feeling of grief which, for some reason, could never be explained.

It was well-known and, without a doubt, one of the best facilities within the state insofar as medical skill and care, where the pauper was treated equally as well as the governor. Nevertheless, it was at the University of Kentucky Medical Center that I found an uneasy feeling of sorrow and grief.

Men in overalls, often with little children, walked to-and-fro in front of the huge hospital, bewildered and frightened. Poor people who were good people, worried about what the doctors might tell them.

One memory I will never forget, and it will haunt me as long as I live.

One day, returning to my car in the hospital parking lot, I noticed an old man, perhaps sixty, sitting on the grass outside the hospital. Surrounding him, with heads bowed and sobbing uncontrollably, were seven men, ranging in age from fifteen to forty. I paused for a moment, and then, I, too, felt their deep sorrow, presuming that his wife, and their mother, had just passed away.

I wanted so much to be of some help, to let them know that someone cared; but, silently, I turned away and walked to my car, knowing that scenes like this were destined to be a part of my life for as long as I continued to be a minister.

15

In semimary, one had the idea that a minister remained in his study throughout the week reading Ephesians; then, on Sunday, he preached a sermon, both notable and uplifting, one that would be remembered. By this inaccessibility, by this aloofness, he became sacrosanct, a respected pillar within the community.

In reality, this is *not* the ministry.

The first thing I did after arriving at Cow Creek was to build a bridge. *Construction* had not been taught at seminary. Jokingly, we called it the Baptist bridge because it was determined to get under water and, indeed, it eventually did.

A minister's job is to minister. When one enters the mission field, it is well to remember that a minister does not preach just once on Sunday. Usually, he preaches three or four times on Sunday. He is also called upon to direct the choir, play the piano, and visit the sick—even though the hospital may be ninety-two miles away.

Other duties include conducting youth meetings, building churches, repairing roofs, hosting the visiting youth groups, and keeping financial records.

He also writes thank-you letters for boxes and gifts received, gives tennis lessons, writes newspaper articles, participates in school activities, settles disputes and attends numerous committee meetings.

Then, too, he must go out on speaking engagements, perform marriages and conduct funerals. The more he becomes entrenched within the community, the more hours he will be involved in counseling. He also finds himself driving more than two thousand miles each month, alternating between a car, a truck, a church van and a Jeep.

During his early ministry, there is a period of adjustment. One Sunday I held the service over on Lower Buffalo. During my prayer, which followed the Scripture reading, one man with a loud voice cried out, "Amen."

"Amen?"

Immediately, I brought my prayer to a close, thinking that this was a signal for me to stop, that the man was tired of my praying. This was not the case, however. I was later to learn that, in our area, when someone shouted the word "Amen," it was simply a sign of approval—of endorsement!

Through the years, this one word, when cried out while I was preaching, always left me completely frustrated. No matter how diligently I had worked on my sermon, no matter how many hours had been spent in the preparation, if, during the delivery, someone cried one "Amen," I completely lost all line of thinking.

One elderly lady, at the Indian Creek Church, quite often would shout "Amen" when I had given a good sermon and *if* she liked it—after which I could not regain my composure.

At her funeral, standing by the casket for the committal service, I repeated the words "Earth to earth, ashes to ashes, dust to dust, in the sure and certain hope of the resurrection to eternal life; through Jesus Christ our Lord. Amen." With special emphasis, and with special significance, I pronounced the "Amen" with a sure and final ring!

During my years in Kenctuky, I could never accept

"Amen," nor could I ever accept a liking for groundhog, cushaw, and shuck beans!

Shuck beans is a favorite dish of Kentucky. Everyone loves shuck beans. They have become sacred. To make a derogatory remark about shuck beans is like talking about a man's dog. It simply is not done!

In looking back over the years, I was to grow in many ways and my outlook on life was to change drastically. Once silent and reserved, in time, I began to laugh and joke—or "prank," as they called it—with the local people, but not before paying a price.

At first, their rather crude, and often rude, remarks made me very uncomfortable. After all, I *was* a minister! Why would they tease me about some person I detested? Why would Jerry Wilson state that, being single, I always waited until the men were gone before making my calls to the various houses here on the creek? My face would turn a crimson red. They dearly loved this teasing. And, in time, I learned that if people loved you they would tease you, they would "prank" with you and they would give you "a hard time." However, on the other hand, if you were disliked, you would be completely ignored. That in itself was the saddest of all experiences.

So, my attitude changed. Whereas I still blushed and felt uncomfortable, I knew and appreciated that this teasing was not a sign of disrespect but an indication of affection and love. Strange, but true! And, in time, I even learned to retaliate.

Jerry Wilson worked at the sawmill and every time I stopped by, my face turned red and I would hurry my departure. This all stemmed from his teasing in the past.

One night I went up to Jerry's to visit, but found that the

family had already gone to bed. A box had arrived that day containing women's articles and I had placed it in the back seat of my car. Smiling, I selected a red shoe from the box and very quietly placed it on the floor inside of Jerry's truck.

The next time I saw Jerry he was not his usual smiling self. "It was you, Joe!" he stammered. "I *know* it was you. You almost got me killed." Then he busted out laughing. "When my wife found that woman's shoe that you put in my truck she nearly killed me. I told her that I had absolutely no idea where it came from, but she wouldn't believe me." He paused. "Yep, Joe! You almost got me killed. I swear!"

At last, I had joined the crowd. After that, the teasing and pranking subsided and they all began to talk of more serious things.

At one time I desperately needed some money. I had never in my life borrowed from a bank and wouldn't know where to begin. I simply went to Jerry and asked if I might borrow one hundred dollars.

With no questions asked, he took out his checkbook from the Farmers State Bank, and wrote out a check for that amount.

The one hundred dollars was repaid over a period of almost two years—five dollars at a time.

I remember so vividly the services held in the various churches; I remember those who came to church so faithfully; and I remember making hospital calls to Lexington, Richmond, Winchester, Hazard and Irvine.

Wednesday was the day I usually set aside for hospital calls. If I knew a person was hospitalized, Presbyterian or not, I would visit and offer a prayer. Usually the stay would only be for a few minutes; but, there were also infrequent occasions when the stay would extend into hours—even overnight.

Visits could be either uplifting or depressing. Quite often I would visit a person who was terminally ill, and I would come away feeling strengthened by the depth of such a person's faith and by their beautiful attitudes about life.

Each Wednesday as I prepared to drive to Lexington, ninety-two miles away, there was always the wonderful realization that my lunch that day would be eaten at the Blue Boar in Turfland Mall! The food was excellent, the service was good and the atmosphere was great! Then, merrily, I would be on my way!

Being a minister is a wonderful, joyful blessing; but, it is also a challenge. Each morning for years I stood by the large window in the manse, looked out toward the church and prayed: "Lord, let everything be all right. Let there be no anger, let there be no problems, let there be no animosity. Truly, let me be Thy servant." Then, one day I suddenly realized how utterly selfish this prayer was! No problems? No animosity? That is *why* we are here. God needs us where there is trouble and where there is conflict.

As ministers, we are to minister to the needy; to the erring; to the fallen, and to the wayward. Our boots become muddy and dirty as we trudge among people who have anger, who possess hatred, and the stench of the world fills our nostrils; but, always, we bend over, keeping the back straight, and we have within us the love and the compassion of our Savior, Jesus Christ. We cannot remain at the mountain top! It is imperative that we go down to the people. We remember the admonition of our Savior, *Be of good cheer* and the words of the psalmist, *Great peace have they which love Thy law and nothing shall offend them.*

Patience is a wonderful virtue and one moves, not by miles nor feet but often by inches. Through our problems, disappointments, and failures, we have always managed to smile and to remember *noblesse oblige*.

Finally, as I stand here alone, my thoughts go out to a beautiful girl of long ago. She was talented, she was brilliant, she possessed all that one would want in a wife, and she was especially gifted to be a minister's wife.

Her idea of success was growth. We would stay at Cow Creek for a few years—five at the most. Then we would seek a larger congregation with more prestige. Her firm belief and conviction was the more successful the minister, the larger the congregation. One simply did not stand still, one moved—always upward and beyond the present situation.

There was the difference of opinion, the different philosophies and, so, with love and with admiration, we parted and went our separate ways.

I do not know where you are, now that your husband has retired; but you are always in my thoughts and in my dreams. Never a day goes by but I remember the softness of your hair, the beauty of your face, your smile, your deep faith, and your dedication to the church.

How well I remember your return to Cow Creek some years ago. Few words were spoken. You had married a Presbyterian minister you said, and in the statistics of our church I followed your climb to success. Your dream of greatness and success had come true; but, that day, you came back alone. There was sadness in your face, in your eyes, and in your voice.

I will always love you. You will never leave my mind, my heart, or my memory.

It is dark now and I dare not tarry any longer. The final

Mary and Belle Eversole.

good-bye, the final farewell, breaks not only the heart but also the mind and the very fiber of the soul. It seems only yesterday that the train left Johnson City, Tennessee, bound for Louisville, Kentucky. It was an overnight journey. I would arrive the next morning at the Louisville Theological Seminary—tall, thin, nervous, and with little money, but with a strong determination that I *would* become a Presbyterian minister. As I walked from the train station to the seminary that morning, little did I know that my life was about to begin, that I was no longer a child but, at last, had become a man!

If only the years could be turned back. If only I could be young once again—timid and awkward—for there is stability in uncertainty, and there is faith in fear. As one grows older and more stable, one loses the thrust for the grail. As we near the top of the mountain, the light somehow becomes not as bright as when we were at the bottom.

But through the years there comes a happiness and a peace that one cannot possess as a novice, for this comes only with and through age. In this hour I feel a sense of accomplishment, a sense of victory, not because I have achieved fame or popular acclaim, but because I have walked among the poor and I have lived among the needy and, in so doing, I have felt wanted. Perhaps *this* is the greatest of all victories.

The people to whom I ministered, contrary to statistics and reports, *were not poor.* Though often clad in overalls, reserved in quiet dignity, and low in material blessings, they were rich in wisdom and in love for each other. Their faith in God was great; their door was always opened to the stranger; they fed the hungry; visited the sick and they gave to a young, stuttering, stammering, minister a cup which truly overflowed.

238

With sadness, I now close the door, leaving behind a valley and a people whom I have loved so deeply.

God bless thee, Cow Creek.

Now unto Him that is able to keep you from falling, and to present you faultless before the presence of His glory with exceeding joy, to the only wise God, our Savior, be glory and majesty, dominion and power, both now and forever. Amen.

The Cow Creek Presbyterian Church today.